W9-BNZ-063

THE
ANTIRACIST
BUSINESS
BOOK

THE
ANTIRACIST
BUSINESS
BOOK

AN EQUITY-CENTERED APPROACH
TO WORK, WEALTH, AND LEADERSHIP

TRUDI LEBRÓN

Copyright © 2022 by Trudi Lebrón

*Row House Publishing recognizes that the power of justice-centered storytelling isn't
a phenomenon; it is essential for progress. We believe in equity and activism, and that
books—and the culture around them—have the potential to transform the universal
conversation around what it means to be human.*

*Part of honoring that conversation is protecting the intellectual property of authors.
Reproducing any portion of this book (except for the use of short quotations for review
purposes) without the expressed written permission of the copyright owner(s) is strictly
prohibited. Submit all requests for usage to rights@rowhousepublishing.com.*

*Thank you for being an important part of the conversation and holding sacred
the critical work of our authors.*

Library of Congress Cataloging-in-Publication Data Available Upon Request
ISBN 978-1-955905-01-5 (HC)
ISBN 978-1-955905-16-9 (eBook)
Printed in the United States
Distributed by Simon & Schuster

Book design by Pauline Neuwirth, Neuwirth & Associates, Inc.

First edition
10 9 8 7 6 5 4 3 2 1

For everyone using their vacation time, sick time,
and lunch breaks to work on their side hustle.
I see you.

You have to act as if it were possible to

radically change the world.

And you have to do it all the time.

ANGELA Y. DAVIS

CONTENTS

FOREWORD
BY ARLAN HAMILTON

I often say you should always be yourself so that the right people can find you. When Trudi Lebron and I found each other, it felt like a true connection. Trudi has been investing in her community since she was a teenager. Her impressive history took her from being a single teen mom with two kids to teaching equity and diversity coaching on how to build antiracist business models. And now, she is adding revolutionary author to the list.

The Anti-Racist Business Book is an informative, empowering tool that will benefit everyone who reads it, whether you're a CEO or an aspiring entrepreneur. Having worked with Trudi, I am amazed by her commitment to racial justice and equitable leadership. Her passion toward bringing antiracism to business has brought a new lens, focusing on how we can transform how we think about work, wealth, and leadership.

As a Black, gay woman who was once homeless and sleeping on airport floors, I am all too familiar with the disparities we, as underestimated members of society, face. I've seen firsthand how racism and capital are linked. It's the reason I built a venture capital fund from the ground up and turned it into a multi-million dollar initiative. In a few years, I went from sleeping in the San Francisco airport to jet-setting from its gates all across the country

Like Trudi, I'm determined to have a massive influence on the business world. My way of doing that is investing in startup companies led by underestimated founders. It was insane to me that 90 percent of venture funding was going to white men. As a person who had no background in finance, even I could see that innovation, motivation, and intelligence were being squandered. The truth is, we don't have to put up with that shit anymore. As the founder and managing partner of Backstage Capital, I am working to minimize these unjust funding disparities in tech by investing in high-potential founders who are BIPOC, women, and LBGT. Trudi's work goes hand in hand with my philosophies on business, opportunity, and talent, which is why I was excited to work with her.

This book isn't just about why we need to create antiracist business practices; it's a deep dive into remixing business, rethinking and reframing how we interact, negotiate, develop, discuss, and define our economic relationships. As Trudi says, "It's not business if it's not personal."

Trudi's vision aligns with my mission, which is to create a world in which generations of wealth are attained and enjoyed by BIPOC, female, and LGBT communities. Our equity in this country is worth trillions of dollars, and it's time to get that money where it belongs. Trudi and I share the common goal of liberating and uplifting the untapped potential in the business world. When we invest in and empower these underestimated sources of innovation and intelligence, we will experience a rich and diverse market full of growth and opportunities for everyone. Just as privilege begets privilege, growth begets growth. We don't have to work for white male bosses for pennies on the dollar anymore. We are becoming the bosses, the deep thinkers, the investors, and the changemakers. And it's about damn time.

By picking up this book, you are uniting with us in our mission to finally paint the future we want to see. You are contributing to a bold, empowered force for change that is unapologetically declaring, *underestimate us if you dare*.

And *The Antiracist Business Book* will show you how.

INTRODUCTION

From the time I was seventeen years old until I graduated at twenty-three, I attended college classes every single semester, including summers. The first few years I took classes part-time, on nights and weekends, because I didn't have childcare during the day. Once my kids were old enough for preschool, at the age of nineteen I enrolled in full-time classes and got a job on campus. My days were grueling. My father would watch me stress out over childcare, money, and my future, offering the best advice he could: "Trudi, why don't you just take a break from school, and get a job at TSA?"

I would look at him totally confused. This man raised me and should have known that there would be no way in the world that I would work for TSA. But his advice was sound. He was watching his daughter, a single mom of two boys, cry at the beginning of every semester because she didn't know if she could do it. He knew, like everybody else, that the chances that I'd actually graduate were slim to none. Out of his best intentions, he was trying to give me an out.

As far as he was concerned, the most secure and stable path he could see was a federal job with the Transportation Security Administration. His selling points were job security, great benefits, a solid health-care plan, and, if I started when I was twenty, early retirement. He'd remind me that once my kids were older, I could go back to school and maybe even get the government to pay for it.

But I knew that if I took even one semester off, I would never go back. I also knew that I was not built to work for people. I was actually a terrible employee, and what made me a terrible employee were the same things that made me a terrible student in school. I asked too many questions, I didn't conform to the status quo, I confronted any perceived injustice, and I had a very low tolerance for arbitrary rules. So, no, TSA was not going to work.

When I was still in college, I started side-hustling as a teaching artist. I taught theater workshops to schoolchildren all over the state of Connecticut for fifty dollars an hour plus mileage. But there is a difference between side-hustling as an artist and building a business. And for a long time I was afraid to build a business because I thought that being a business owner would turn me into a bad person, a money-focused capitalist who would abandon her community. I thought that was the inevitable trade-off—the price of success.

After I graduated and entered the workforce, I found that this narrative was reinforced at every level. My whole career I was constantly doubted and patronized, confronted with advice about dressing more "professionally" if I wanted to be taken seriously, and working in places with racist and homophobic colleagues. I didn't have the power to speak up because my livelihood, and that of my children, was dependent on whatever institution I was working for at the moment. Throughout my career, there were times when I was responsible for upholding an unjust policy and my job was on the line if I tried to do the right thing. Like the time I was written up by my supervisor for feeding a pregnant student who had arrived to school late. I had violated a school policy that said that students who arrived at school after the bell could not eat breakfast. Conventional success in a corporate institution, or the nonprofit space, required a major compromise of my values. And I just couldn't do it anymore.

In 2008, I started doing diversity, equity, and inclusion consulting and training for national organizations, and I saw how even institutions whose central missions of diversity and inclusion also fell into the traps of toxic capitalism, bias, discrimination, exploitation, and compromising the very values that they were trying to instill in others.

What I realized was that even the best intentions got marred in their implementation.

> I knew that there had to be a better way, an approach to how we run our companies and our lives that would create a new paradigm for profit, but also for *all* people.

A paradigm that didn't favor those with the most resources, but rather one that created equitable and reparative opportunities for those with the fewest resources.

The idea for this book is the result of my unlikely life path that includes long stretches of poverty and struggle, navigating the world as a very young teen mother, acquiring a master's degree, progressing through a PhD program (currently ABD) in social psychology, having a very successful career in nonprofit leadership, and building a successful consulting firm and coaching practice. All while practicing my own commitments to antiracism, diversity, inclusion, equity, self-determination, liberation, and justice in my life and business on a daily basis. And, of course, let's not forget our shared struggle of trying to navigate the world we live in, while attempting to build the world that we need.

As part of that practice and commitment, I want to share that even through the hardships and marginalization in my own story, I acknowledge the privileges I've had that impacted my life and were likely key contributions to my ability to overcome tremendous odds. As I write this paragraph, I am sitting on the stolen land of the Podunk people in central Connecticut. I am a light-skinned, cisgender, non-disabled, biracial Latina. I was raised by two parents who were employed. Despite growing up in a bilingual home, I was brought up to predominantly speak English because my parents didn't want me to have to struggle in school because of a language barrier. I am a citizen of the country I reside in, and so are my parents. From the time I was fifteen to the time I was twenty-five, I was a single mother of two, but since then I have had a loving partner and co-parent who is very supportive of my professional and academic pursuits.

I share this as an acknowledgment of the privileges I have and how my privileges have shifted over the years. Privilege has become something people, especially White people, get very uncomfortable thinking about. It's a misconception that just because you hold privileges means that you somehow haven't had to work hard or haven't experienced hardship or trauma. That is not the case. Privilege simply means we have some things, whether those are parts of our identity or access to resources that are working in our favor. Some of those privileges might be things we have because we've earned them, like an education, or if you've earned your way into a higher socioeconomic status. But others are not earned—they are inherent. Your race, being a citizen of the country you reside in, not living with a disability that requires accommodations for you to go about your daily life.

I started encouraging clients to write privilege statements like this as an act of transparency and self-reflection so that they can be mindful of how they are entering the conversation, and so they can give others context about who they are. No single part of our identities defines us, but these parts of our identities do shape our experiences in the world. And our interpretations of those experiences become a lens through which we view ourselves and the world around us.

By owning our identities and privileges, I hope that we become more comfortable engaging in uncomfortable conversations. I hope we become more connected, hold less shame, and relate to one another more honestly.

As antiracist entrepreneurs and leaders, we need to be honest about where our power and privilege comes from, and then we must use that power and privilege to advance antiracist policies and practices in our businesses and workplaces. It's time to move beyond the old conversations about increasing diversity and inclusion. Efforts to increase diversity are rooted in the assumption that the problem with businesses is their lack of diversity. I disagree. I don't think that a lack of diversity is the problem—I think a lack of diversity is the result of systemic racism, White supremacy, and conscious and unconscious bias.

The solution to businesses that are rooted in racism and systemic oppression is not building more diversity on your team or among your clients. It's not about creating an inclusivity policy or mission statement that names your commitment to equity. It's not about your social responsibility initiatives or the Black Lives Matter banner on your website.

The solution is that we become antiracist leaders, entrepreneurs, executives, coaches, service providers, workers, and creators. It's that we see our work as a piece of the puzzle to creating a more equitable world. A world where a person's life outcomes are no longer statistically predictable by their race and their zip code. It requires a transformation of the way we do business.

And that is what this book is all about.

I hope to add to the field of antiracism education and fill a gap in business education literature by exploring how the concepts of antiracism move from theory to practice in the business world. I happen to believe that advancing the concept of business antiracism is a critical step in moving us toward an antiracist (and hopefully, one day, truly post-racial) society. In today's economy, more people are starting businesses, building side-hustles to supplement their income, or operating and acting as contract laborers in the gig economy. An increasing number of people are becoming their own boss, and many of those people are collaborating with other contractors and companies, making the network of entrepreneurs more closely connected than ever before. Some are lucky enough to be able to create jobs. This means we have two choices: we can continue to perpetuate business practices that are oppressive and exploitative, or we can figure out a new way. We can build businesses that are as profitable as they are liberatory and just.

We have a choice between business as usual, or building an equity-centered, antiracist approach to business. In this book, we're going to unpack and explore how to negotiate these choices in how we work, lead, and understand wealth. I want to be clear that any work having to do with antiracism is an imperfect practice. I can't guarantee that if you follow every bit of advice in this book that you will never make a mistake, never offend someone, never cause harm, or never negatively impact someone. In fact, anyone making a claim that their way of doing something is the one and only right way, or the guaranteed path to any particular outcome, is not engaging in an equity-centered, antiracist practice. Antiracism is something we must collectively commit to exploring and building together, and not something to which any one person can guarantee a road map.

The fact remains that we don't live in an equitable world. The capitalist system we have was literally built on the backs of enslaved people and exploited laborers. We have been and continue to be educated in separate and unequal schools and communities. We can send people to space, we have self-driving cars, we walk around with powerful computers in our pockets, but we have not been able to create a world in which people have equitable access to housing, jobs, food, education, or work. We have a lot of work to do. But the good news is that we all have the chance to participate in it.

In her book *Emergent Strategy*, adrienne maree brown, author, thought leader, and facilitator, writes: "Science fiction is simply a way to practice the future together. I suspect that is what many of you are up to, practicing futures together, practicing justice together, living into new stories. It is our right and responsibility to create a new world."[1]

This book seeks to be exactly that: partially a critique of what we have, and part strategic advice for how to move toward a more just, equitable, and antiracist entrepreneurship, work, and life. But it is also part science fiction in that we are imagining a world of business and work that is radically different from what we've inherited.

This book is for you if you're frustrated because the advice you've been getting about how to build a successful business is in conflict with your values, your beliefs, and your access to resources. It's for you if you're a business leader feeling like the policies and practices you have created, or have been asked to uphold and enforce, feel outdated or arbitrary, or maybe you realize that the consequences of those policies and practices impact people inequitably. Maybe you're looking to improve your workplace culture, or to improve your retention of high-quality team members or your best clients. Maybe you've been called out, or have seen someone be called out, and you're trying to figure out how to avoid making the same mistakes.

This book is also for you if you identify as an antiracist, activist, ally, accomplice, or co-conspirator to the movement of racial justice and you're trying to negotiate change in the workplace. You might even see yourself as an anti-capitalist looking to reconcile the need to engage in business and earn money, while rejecting the fundamental underpinnings of capitalist society.

Or maybe you're a skeptic. Maybe you've picked up this book because you're committed to finding all the ways in which the ideas you find in here won't work. This book can also be for you. If there is one thing I can tell you, it's that a person can't do the work I've done over the course of my twenty-year career working to improve the lives of other humans if they didn't genuinely believe that people can grow and change. Humans, for the most part, are fundamentally good, but many have been taught behaviors, mindsets, and ways of being that cause harm—sometimes the kind of harm that lasts generations. Yet without the belief that there is a path forward, the work I do would not make any sense. And so, to the skeptics, I hope this book offers you the truth you did not realize you were seeking.

COMMUNITY AGREEMENTS

The practice of setting agreements or guidelines is discussed in depth in Chapter 7. But I'd like to set some agreements here that reflect the intentions with which I've tried to approach this book and to create an intentional space for you to take in the ideas and information:

- **This book is not a "perfect" road map to a perfect anti-racist practice. There is no such thing.** Perfectionism is a function of Whiteness that becomes a distraction to real progress. I hold a lot of expertise in this work, which means that I offer a lot of ideas and advice. You might find other antiracism and DEI practitioners who disagree with me, similar to how two different doctors might suggest a different course of treatment for the same disease. We have the right to have differences of opinion and approaches in our discipline the same way that other professions do. If you read something here that is a different message than what you've heard elsewhere, it doesn't make either approach wrong. It just means that there is more than one way to approach a problem, and now you have options.

■ **Try on these concepts.** I can tell you right now that I will propose some ideas in this book that you might think are ridiculous. At one point, I even thought that some of them were so outside of the box that they would never work. If and when that happens, I simply ask you to "try on" these ideas. Imagine what it would be like to implement them. Imagine what it would be like if your boss or supervisor implemented them. Mostly, ask "Why would someone want to do this?" and "What larger shift or change does it contribute to?" You don't have to agree with these ideas, but I do ask that you at least deeply consider the ideas that you resist the most.

■ **This book was written in the spring and summer of 2021 and reflects the language and dominant needs of this moment.** Issues and language in the antiracism space change rapidly. Depending on when you read this book, language may have evolved and issues may have altered. I ask for your grace if terminology has shifted by the time the book reaches your hands, or if you have a different understanding or context for language that is not included here. Please know that I have put a lot of effort into being as intentional and inclusive as possible. Some of the language I use in this book includes the following:

- **BIPoC:** This acronym stands for "Black/Brown, Indigenous, and People of Color." This term in this book includes all Black, Brown, Latine, Asian, Pacific Islander, Indigenous peoples, Middle Eastern, and all non-White identifying folks. I also move between terms "Black/Brown," "People of Color," and "BIPoC" to mean non-White folks. There are places in this book where I reference Black Americans specifically because, of all BIPoC communities, Black Americans have experienced unique generational trauma, exploitation, and racial marginalization in the name of White supremacy that is distinct from the experiences of others.

● **Latine:** I have chosen to use the term "Latine," which is a nongendered form of the words "Latino" and "Latina." I am using "Latine" over "Latinx" because of conversations happening in both the queer/trans communities regarding the use of the letter "x" being an inappropriate expression of inclusivity, and also among language experts who agree that "Latine" is a more natural evolution of language.

● **LGBTQIA2S+:** I use this acronym for "Lesbian, Gay, Bisexual/Bicurious, Trans, Queer, Intersex, Asexual, Two-Spirit plus" as an acknowledgment that this list is incomplete and will likely continue to evolve. I have been involved in recent conversations that identified the need for language that disconnects gender identities from sexual orientation. I want readers to know that I understand this difference and the limitations of the current acronym and am waiting and learning as trans and nonbinary folks guide us to move forward with the evolution of language over time.

● **Brad, Chad, and Karen archetypes:** These names are used as archetypes for White men and women

who are either oblivious to their Whiteness or wea-
ponize it. If your name is Brad, Chad, or Karen,
know that this is not a reference to you personally—
unless you do actually embody the archetype.

Hopefully these agreements provide you with a bit of insight
into my intentions for this book, and how I hope for you to experience it. If you'd like more resources for this book, please go to
www.antiracistbusinessbook.com, where you can find business
tools, activities, and supports to create and reframe your business
through an antiracist lens. I want you to be inspired and uncomfortable, to learn new things and to confirm other things you've
thought and felt. I want you to feel like you can be part of the
solution to building a better way of doing business by taking action in your own company or workplace. And I want you to win.
I want us all to win. Success is not a zero-sum game, and neither
is our liberation.

THE
ANTIRACIST
BUSINESS
BOOK

PART 1

ANTIRACIST BUSINESS IN A CAPITALIST SYSTEM

I can't name a single issue with roots in race that doesn't have economic implications, and I cannot think of a single economic issue that doesn't have racial implications. The idea that we have to separate them is a con.

ALEXANDRIA OCASIO-CORTEZ

CHAPTER 1

WHITE PEOPLE SHIT

On a cold February day in 2016, I sat at my desk in the community-based nonprofit organization where I worked as the assistant director of family and youth programming, refreshing my browser every thirty seconds waiting for the next batch of World Domination Summit tickets to be available for purchase. I had been dreaming of attending WDS for two years. The previous year I missed out because I didn't know that tickets sold as if they were for a Beyoncé concert, and by the time I came up with the seven hundred dollars for a ticket, it was too late, and I certainly wasn't connected enough to purchase a ticket from someone who would no longer be able to go.

Just a few years before, the idea of spending hundreds of dollars of my own money on a ticket to a conference—and hundreds more to travel across the country, from Hartford, Connecticut, to Portland, Oregon, to attend—wasn't something I could even wrap my mind around. As far as I was concerned, that was White People Shit, and not something that someone like me—a poor, biracial,

teen mom who had been on food stamps and housing subsidies—
would ever be able to do.

Where I come from, "White People Shit" (WPS) is a catch-all
phrase that encompasses all the things that White people do because of a combination of privilege, access, historical precedent,
social norms, and the general ability to do what they want just
because it fits their social script. To be honest, we also use the
phrase to describe a set of behaviors and practices that we just
don't understand—like putting fruit in potato salad, or allowing
children to cuss and throw tantrums in supermarkets. Obviously,
not all White people engage in these behaviors, but consider the
feelings you're having right now as you read this. If you are a
White person, it might feel really strange to hear descriptions of
White people that are basically inaccurate stereotypes, but it's
only uncomfortable because you are not used to hearing those
kinds of remarks being made about White people.

As far as I could tell, attending World Domination Summit was
definitely some White People Shit because it had all the trappings,
including:

- Corny activities like breaking a Guinness World Record
  for the largest breakfast in bed and having opening
  parties at a zoo
- Very enthusiastic White people cheering and giving high
  fives and hugs to complete strangers (just weird)
- A name like "World Domination Summit," which is
  definitely something only White people could ever get
  away with
- Lots of White people . . . hundreds and hundreds of
  White folks in photos all over the conference's website
  and social media

But as far as I was concerned, these White people knew something that I needed to know. I needed to know how to free myself from my 9:00 a.m. to 7:00 p.m. nonprofit career, where I was perpetually one paycheck away from homelessness, and turn my consulting side-hustle into a full-time business that I could run from anywhere in the world; if I could do it in a four-hour work-week, even better. My understanding was that the White people that were going to World Domination Summit had figured it out, and I was going to learn their secret.

So I sat there, refreshing my screen, debit card in hand, waiting to make a purchase that I hoped would change my life. A few minutes later I would post to Twitter, "I got a Golden (WDS) ticket!!!"

WDS changed my life. Not in the exact way I expected it to, but it spun me on a journey where my commitment to diversity, equity, inclusion, and antiracism intersected with my obsession with personal growth (not to mention my legitimate need for financial success). I came home from Portland and gave my employer notice that I would be leaving in six months. I was going to be a full-time entrepreneur.

What's interesting about that experience at my first WDS in 2016 was that most of my fears were confirmed. It was definitely and overwhelmingly a White space—eight out of nine of the mainstage speakers were White. There were countless microaggressions, stereotypes, and the classic overemphasis of using privileges that most White people take for granted as key components of success. I remember sitting in the auditorium listening to speaker after speaker share a variation of a similar story. They quit their jobs, sold everything they owned, and spent a year facing their fears, traveling the world, blogging, building an audience, and launching a business. Then they wrote a book about it. Of course, each speaker had a personal narrative that was touching and meaningful, and yet, as I watched speaker after speaker, I just couldn't find myself in their stories. I remember shifting in my seat, trying to glean any drops of information and inspiration that could apply to my life, as a thirty-four-year-old mother of three, with six-figures of school debt, no savings, and a cultural context that didn't consider selling all my possessions to become a digital nomad a viable option. I couldn't do a friends-and-family round of fundraising, I couldn't take out a loan . . . shit, I couldn't even get a credit card.

But of course WDS would be a majority White space. What I would learn over the next few years of my entrepreneurial journey was that WDS was just a microcosm of the larger entrepreneurship, online business, personal development world and was seeping patterns of what bell hooks describes as imperialist, White supremacist, capitalist patriarchy.[1]

One stroll through the business section of the bookstore and you will find a mix of old-school corporate approaches to business, with an overwhelming dose of motivational, "no-nonsense" straight talk, all with catchy titles and road maps promising success if you just follow a simple formula of waking up at the ass-crack of dawn, regular meditation, green juice, being an early adopter of every social media platform out there, outsourcing everything, committing to an "abundant" lifestyle—including spending money you don't have, in order to make more money—and, let's not forget, prioritizing your own self-care.

If I didn't know any better and wasn't who I was, I would have picked up some harmful narratives about the nature of entrepreneurship based on most of my early experiences in this journey. Those lessons would have included the following.

■ **Personal development, money, and status are linked, and personal development is White People Shit.** This is evidenced by the kinds of books that show up in Google and Amazon searches for personal development, including business books like *The 4-Hour Workweek* by Tim Ferris, Dale Carnegie's *How to Win Friends and Influence People*, and influencers like Rachel Hollis whose mix of business coaching, inspiration, and life advice has skyrocketed to the top of the *New York Times* bestseller list and a multimillion-dollar brand. These books, thought leaders, and audiences are overwhelmingly White.

■ **The power to change your life lies within you . . . if you are White.** Books like Tony Robbins's *Awaken the Giant Within*, Louise Hay's *You Can Heal Your Life*, the more recent *You Are a Badass* series by Jen Sincero, and titles like *Unfu*k Yourself* by Gary John Bishop all send the strong message that the answers and transformations you seek are already inside of you. This is a stark contrast from the messages that Black and Brown folks receive about change needing to be facilitated by some outside source—a teacher, a social worker, God.

■ **There is a difference between a side-hustle and being a successful entrepreneur, and entrepreneurship is White People Shit.** Every one of the early business books I read and early programs I participated in shared a few impossibilities for me. They wanted me to write a long business plan with financial models, funding plans, pitch decks, blah blah blah. And most of the advice offered—to live off credit cards (which I didn't have and couldn't get), borrow money from friends and family (they ain't got it), reduce my monthly living expenses to near nothing, as if qualifying for food stamps and housing subsidies didn't imply that I was already at the bare minimum—was negligible, if not negligent.

This short list is full of countercultural messages that boil down to "Not for Us," including the fact that many of us, including myself, were taught that (White) people with lots of money are bad, that money is always hard to earn, and that it's definitely not realistic to earn what you need in four hours a week unless you're running a scam. Also, from my vantage point, it seemed like the history of the world is 100 percent invested in perpetuating the message that something is inherently wrong with Black and Brown communities, especially the community I was raised in, and that we all need saving from the outside.

The dominant narrative of my childhood and adolescence was that my friends and I were "bad," and that we were destined for tragedy (jail, teen pregnancy, drugs, and death) unless the generous intervention of a well-meaning White person worked in our favor.

> The idea that we had answers or some sort of power inside of us that could be activated to unleash success was unthinkable. That kind of confidence was for White folks.

Or so we have been made to believe. You see, there shouldn't be such a thing as White People Shit. If you're new to this conversation, you might even be thinking: *What kind of world do we live in that some things are designated as "for White people"? Isn't that also racist?*

Why, yes, it most definitely is racist. But not in the way you might be thinking. People who grow up in communities like mine have an awareness that some shit is not for us because of a combination of lived experience of various types of marginalization and lack of access to quality education, affordable housing, living-wage jobs, comprehensive health care, fresh, affordable, healthy foods, and even just the environmental difference in the spaces we occupy.

I remember being nineteen years old and riding the city bus from the South End of Hartford to the mall where I worked part-time a few towns over. My favorite bus route to take was the E bus. This bus ran less frequently than some of the other mall routes and took longer to get to its final destination, but when I had the option to take it, I would. The E bus would travel down Farmington Avenue in Hartford, pass pristine insurance campuses like Aetna and The Hartford, and drive down a few blocks into the neighborhood where I first attended high school. There you would find an array of dollar stores, high-counter Chinese and pizza restaurants, a Taco Bell, a laundromat, and several bodegas, before eventually driving into the West End of Hartford where the neighborhood started to change from multi-unit apartment buildings with absentee landlords to townhomes and condos that, though they structurally looked the same as the buildings a few blocks away, were marked by beautifully manicured lawns, well-lit entrances, and signs in the front of the buildings displaying names like "The Packard."

The E bus would continue straight over the town line into West Hartford, and the farther away we got from regular Hartford, the cleaner the streets got, the nicer the buildings became, and the more and more White people you saw driving their cars, walking their dogs, pushing strollers, and smiling. Even the White people who got on and off the bus had a different vibe to them. They didn't have the same look of exhaustion and despair that those of us who got on the bus in Hartford had. Women wore comfy running shoes and had a plain black backpack slung over their shoulder. They made taking the bus look like a leisurely way to beat traffic after a long day at the office, instead of what it was for me: my only transportation option, and one I would take several times a day to shuffle my kids and me between home, day care, school, work, grocery shopping, doctor's appointments, welfare appointments, and anything else that had to get done.

But I loved taking the E bus to the mall because we would drive by a shopping district called West Hartford Center. Even though

West Hartford Center was only six-and-a-half miles from the house I lived in for most of my adolescent life, I had never seen it before until I took that first bus ride on the E line, and it would be a few years before I was comfortable walking down the sidewalk there. For years, I would ride the bus and look out the window at stores I couldn't afford, the people eating on the patios at the kinds of restaurants that I'd never been to, and people not walking, but strolling up and down the streets, not going anywhere in particular. They were just out enjoying themselves and each other. There were teenagers, my age and younger, who were just hanging out. Sitting on benches, laughing, smiling, being loud teenagers, and no one was bothering them. No one told them that they couldn't be there. That kind of freedom and leisure was for White people.

Riding the E bus from Downtown Hartford to West Hartford gave me a short peek into a world that wasn't mine. We didn't have spaces like this. The cheap strip malls that we did have were not welcoming. There were no ice cream parlors or teen-friendly cafés, no benches to sit on, and if we propped ourselves up against a lamp pole or cinder block, people would look at us as though we were up to something. Our spaces had trash strewn around the huge, mostly empty parking lots and there was little to no landscaping. These were not the kinds of places where people took leisurely walks. Now that I think about it, I actually don't remember anyone going for leisurely walks. We walked because we had to get places. The fanciest restaurant I was eating in was a Chinese buffet that served all the standards and a couple of "fancy" options like boiled crab legs, and in order to get any you had to hover around the seafood station waiting for someone to bring out a new batch of crab legs from the kitchen, because as soon as they were served they would be gone.

For centuries now, we have lived in a world where one of the biggest determining factors of a person's life outcome is their race.

I wish that weren't true, but it is. There is extensive research documenting the life, wealth, education, and health disparities between White people and non-White people. Based on a person's race and zip code (and zip code and race being inextricably linked because of redlining, housing policies, and income levels), demographers and other social scientists can predict, with a good deal of accuracy, the likelihood that someone will graduate high school, attend and complete college, get married, make a certain amount of money, and understand what kinds of health problems they might encounter during their lifetime.

Here we are, in 2022, and for the most part we've accepted that there is no biological basis for race. In other words, there are no biological differences between races that explain these disparities. They are not natural. This also means that the disparities that do exist are completely socially constructed and reinforced in our social systems. These systems are then reinforced by policies and practices that create a self-sustaining system of marginalization and oppression. Policies that prevented Black and Brown folks from living in certain neighborhoods and prevented them from sending their children to schools that were better resourced, because other policies were created to fund the education system based on property taxes. The disparities are by design, and so the things that White people get to do because of that design are accessible to them based on their race. This turns into a cycle of policy and practice, and causes the internalization of these narratives. "White kids go to good schools; good schools are not for me. We are not worthy of good schools; I am not good."

> Inequity is built in and reinforced by just about every space and environment we encounter, unless there has been an intentional disruption, a dismantling of the status quo, *and* (the "and" part is critical) a way of replacing it with new ways of being.

But how? How do you break and replace a system that so many people have bought into? How do you convince people that we need to do things differently in order to better support the people who are the most disenfranchised when the people who need to do the shifting are those who hold the power? How do you teach people that it is in the best interest of us all if we find better solutions when some people feel like these solutions require them to give up something to which they are entitled? How do you encourage Black and Brown folks to divest from the policies and practices that they had to uphold in order to "make it" because the systems are fundamentally oppressive and exploitative?

White People Shit is the upholding and replicating of the policies, practices, behaviors, and ideas that perpetuate Whiteness, disproportionately impacting folks whose identities have been marginalized, creating inequity, modeling colonialism, appropriating culture, and exploiting labor. And these practices can be upheld by all people, not just White people.

What's important to understand is that "Whiteness" and "White people" are not identical concepts. "White people" merely means "people who are White." "Whiteness" refers to the cultural practices, ideologies, traditions, language, historical context, and, more recently, political priorities that can be traced to White supremacy because these cultural ways of being and political agendas disproportionately punish communities of Color.

The misconception that only White people can replicate or uphold Whiteness is often a point of frustration for non-White people who hold what is often described as "conservative values" because it can be a way to easily dismiss them as being "not really Black" or "not (fill in the non-White identity) enough." Many people feel like talking or teaching about topics like Whiteness or critical race theory teaches White people to be ashamed of who they are and teaches Black and Brown folks that White people are the reason for everything wrong in their lives. These are misunderstandings and oversimplifications of very nuanced systems and social relationships. What is truer is that the more we understand about each other, our history, and our systems, the more equipped we are to find solutions. The more comfortable we become in these uncomfortable conversations, the better we are able to communicate our feelings and our dreams for the future, and to work collaboratively to create a new, equitable, just system. The more we are willing to leave our egos at the door, the better we are able to share power, learn from each other, and be willing to engage in generative conflict—even if that means we don't always get it right.

White People Shit is the opposite of that. It's the belief that you are inherently good and that you are right all the time. It's the desire to justify mistakes instead of taking accountability and repairing harm. It's the consolidation of power and resources and the privileging of arbitrary markers of acceptability and success. It's also the replication of the toxic practices of capitalism and the controlling of people's time, will, land, and ideas. Ultimately, it's the weaponizing of authority, like police, courts, lawyers, contracts, security guards, HR departments, state and local governmental offices, and even neighborhood watchmen.

You might be wondering, *What does any of this have to do with building an antiracist business? When do we start talking about sales and marketing?* I promise we'll get to that, but one of the foundational requirements of any antiracist practice is to understand how we got to where we are. If we are on a path toward antiracist business, then we have to explore how Whiteness and racism are often upheld by the institutions we create, including our individual businesses, whether those are small mom-and-pop outfits or large corporations. Institutions might uphold systemic racism, but people build institutions, and there is an important opportunity to disrupt, dismantle, and rebuild new systems through the choices we make when creating businesses, leading teams, and engaging in daily interactions with each other. We have to be willing to sit with the possibility that even though you don't think you are racist, or you are a Black, Brown, Indigenous, Latine, Middle Eastern, South Asian, Pacific Islander, or other non-White identity, that you (and I!) might just be participating in practices that continue to marginalize People of Color.

But in order to understand the widespread impact of racism in this world, we have to understand its history, especially as an underpinning of the basic mechanics of our present economy. The world as we know it didn't just appear out of hard work and good intentions. The land we live on was settled with literal blood, the bulk of our modern-day conveniences continue to be produced by unethical labor, and the entire economic system of the Western world was crafted through and fueled by the four hundred years of slavery that formed most of our current political and cultural belief systems. This isn't just White People Shit; this is All People Shit. And it affects every single one of us—from the Brads and Chads running the companies, to the Karens in HR, to the people in the field. In denying our history, we are only compromising our future. As business owners, we have to understand the deep and embedded threads of systemic racism before we can begin to unravel them.

CHAPTER 2

IS BUSINESS RACIST?

As shocking as it might be to some people who became aware of antiracism and diversity, equity, and inclusion work after the murder of George Floyd in 2020, when social uprisings spilled onto the streets and into our social media streams, the goal of antiracism work is not to create nicer White people. Less racist White people is absolutely an outcome, but the ultimate goal of antiracism is equity. We live in a world where people's race is a primary indicator of their life outcomes, impacting the everyday interactions that many people have throughout their lives, every single day. The goal of antiracism is to end this. Permanently. Ibram X. Kendi defines an antiracist as a person who "is supporting an antiracist policy through their actions or expressing an antiracist idea."[1]

Antiracism is the practice of creating, supporting, advocating, and carrying out policies, practices, worldviews, and ideologies that dismantle all forms of racism, oppression, and exploitation, and reinforce equity so that we live in a world where people's race or any other aspects of their identity are not predictors of their life outcomes. This would mean living in a society where people have access to all the things they need in order to live happy, healthy, safe, and meaningful lives. Where there is true representation in all levels of society and government, and where children have access to high-quality education regardless of where they live.

I believe that antiracist business has the potential to make monumental shifts toward the larger goals of antiracism because most of us engage with businesses every day. We are consumers, clients, workers, leaders, CEOs, executive directors, board members, advisors, and family members of all of these groups of people. Businesses have the decision-making power to create economic equity or exploit economic fragility. We have the ability to provide health care, and we have the ability to impact people's schedules and work responsibilities. We can build a culture built on trust and community, or on distrust and individualism. Many of us also have political power and the ability to support candidates that will align with antiracist values or reinforce racist ones.

| The goals of antiracism are equity and justice.

Over the course of more than twenty years of experience as an ambitious woman trying to carve out a place for herself in the world, I've often wondered what needed to happen in this world so that I wasn't considered a statistical minority of success, but rather a commonplace story. The answer to that question depends on who you ask. But you've picked up a book called *The Antiracist Business Book*, after all, so you can probably guess my answer. As I hope you'll find as you get to know me over the course of this book, my approach isn't based on a gut instinct or even my personal journey. Even though those things have led me to the same conclusions, it's important that we look at the facts. So, let's do that.

EMPLOYMENT AND UNEMPLOYMENT

It's no secret that the American economy was built by the enslavement of millions of humans, forced to work without pay and under extreme violence and duress in order to execute the Industrial Revolution, which established America's wealth and prominence in the world. Slavery wasn't abolished in America until 1865, over four hundred years after the first public sale of Africans in Lagos, Portugal. For four hundred years (take that in, friends), slavery was the system under which the Americas were built.

And since 1865, a mere 155 years ago, the American economy has been further strengthened by occupational segregation and government policies that exclude BIPoC. And yes, our history of slavery, segregation, and exclusionary policies still affects the workplace today, benefiting White people and exploiting marginalized labor. Colonization, slavery, Jim Crow, and the New Deal fueled White supremacy and destroyed equality in America. Additionally, antidiscrimination agencies have consistently had their hands tied due to legal battles, loopholes, and legislation, making progress excruciatingly slow, if not impossible. Poor policy decisions designed to keep workers of Color down, stuck in undervalued jobs, and making less in wages and benefits than their White coworkers, if they get hired at all, are continuing today to contribute to our country's ongoing inequality problem. Due to historical and perpetual bigotry in America, racial disparities are still prevalent in today's job markets.

To fully understand how our history is still impacting our present circumstances with regard to employment, we must go through a brief timeline of America's history of exploitation and exclusion. Let's start with slavery. For those 421 years, Black people were forced into slavery, working in atrocious and inhumane conditions, to do back-breaking, undervalued jobs for White people, such as domestic services and agricultural labor. According to an article in *Social Science Quarterly*, the value in 2009 of U.S. slave labor ranged from $5.9 to $14.2 trillion dollars.[2] But that was a long time ago, right? Well, the exploitation didn't stop when slavery was abolished.

The abolishment of slavery in 1865 did not allow Black people to work in any occupation they wanted. The Freedman's Bureau, which was a government agency created to help previously enslaved people transition to freedom, encouraged freed slaves to continue working in the South with the same families that had formerly enslaved them, but this time as paid staff.[3] Jim Crow laws came quickly on the heels of Reconstruction, putting a chokehold on the liberation of formerly enslaved Black people as early as 1865.[4] Emigrant-agent laws made it illegal for employers in Northern states to recruit workers or fund the relocation of Black employees from the South. Black Codes, which were oppressive state and local laws, determined which jobs Black people could hold, where they could work, and the maximum wage they were allowed to earn. This limited Black people to low-paying jobs in farming or domestic labor.[5] Jim Crow and Black Code laws also made it a crime for Black people to be unemployed. They called it vagrancy. Since the police and judges were all former Confederate soldiers, the law discriminated heavily against Black people. This led to the mass incarceration of Black people who, thanks to a loophole in the Thirteenth Amendment that states that involuntary servitude can only exist as punishment for a crime, were forced back into unpaid labor on the very plantations where they were formerly enslaved.[6]

The terror of the Jim Crow South caused many Black families to flee to the Northern states. This exodus left Southerners searching for low-wage laborers of Color in domestic and agriculture fields. They turned to Latine and Asian populations to fill those jobs. There is still evidence of this today. Those in low-paying service, domestic, and agriculture jobs are largely People of Color. According to the Center for American Progress, "While Black or African American, Asian, and Hispanic or Latino people comprise 36 percent of the overall U.S. workforce, they constitute 58 percent of miscellaneous agricultural workers; 70 percent of maids and housekeeping cleaners; and 74 percent of baggage porters, bellhops, and concierges."[7] One only needs to open their eyes and look around to see the results of our history in the overwhelming numbers of BIPoC workers in low-wage jobs.

Oppression, inequality, and exclusion in the workforce didn't stop with slavery and Jim Crow laws. During the Great Depression, African Americans were disproportionately impacted by unemployment and poverty. They were commonly the first to be fired and the last to be hired.[8] After the Great Depression, the New Deal lifted families out of devastating poverty and gave them access to upward economic mobility. Employment rates went up and workers enjoyed higher wages and benefits for their labor. In reality, the New Deal mainly targeted and benefited White families and White workers, largely excluding BIPoC workers. This exclusion still affects people today. Under the New Deal, the Fair Labor Standards Act (FLSA) of 1938 ensured safe and fair working conditions for America's labor force, except the FLSA conveniently forgot to include domestic, agricultural, and service jobs in their bubble of protection.[9] As we know from previous research, BIPoC workers are disproportionately represented in those fields. In 1935, the National Labor Relations Act, also known as the Wagner Act, which was implemented to increase bargaining rights for unions, also excluded domestic and agricultural fields.

According to the U.S. Bureau of Labor Statistics, the African American unemployment rate has consistently been twice as high as the White unemployment rate for the last five decades, except in the few months after the Great Recession of 2008.[10] Between 1973 and 2018, the unemployment rate for African Americans has remained at or above twice the White unemployment rate.[11] That unemployment disparity is wider in metropolitan areas with higher Black populations. According to the Brookings Institution, the African American unemployment rate in Washington, D.C., is six times higher than the White unemployment rate.[12]

Additionally, states that have a higher Black population tend to have less generous unemployment benefits.[13] When Black workers are forced into unemployment, they can't get the help they need to get back on their feet, contributing to further unemployment and hardship. The Black/White unemployment gap stretches across all fields, education levels, and ages. The mass incarceration of Black people plays a large role in unemployment, as a criminal record significantly limits job prospects.[14] There is also a disparity in labor force participation between White women and Black women. Black women are more likely to be in lower-paying jobs, even though they represent a higher rate of participation in the workforce than White women.[15]

> It may feel more comfortable to hide America's sins in the darkest corners of history, never to examine or discuss them. However, that history is seeping into our present and affecting our everyday lives.

Systemic racism is, by design, woven into every part of our society. It is enmeshed, and therefore difficult to repair by merely pulling one or two threads. Slavery, Jim Crow, and economic exclusion and oppression are the foundation of our American system. This inequality affects not only employment rates but also earning potential and generational wealth.

EARNINGS AND WEALTH

Considering all of this evidence of employment inequality for People of Color in this country, it's logical that there would also be an income and wealth gap. According to the Brookings Institute, in 2019, the median White household had about $188,200 in wealth.[16] This is 7.8 times higher than the median Black household, which averaged $24,100. The scale of average wealth, which factors in the households with the greatest amounts of wealth, is higher. White households hold a 6.9 times higher average of wealth, at $983,400, while Black households hold $142,500. An overview from the Federal Reserve showed that in the second quarter of 2020, even though White households accounted for 60 percent of the U.S. population, they held 84 percent of total household wealth ($94 trillion).[17] By contrast, Black households, who accounted for 13.4 percent of the U.S. population, only held 4 percent of total household wealth ($4.6 trillion). The American economy has long been functioning on a system that limits income and opportunities for BIPoC communities, and its consequences ripple throughout these communities every day.

In 2019, the median hourly wage in the United States was $18.58.[18] But those in the service industry, which as we know are comprised of a higher percentage of Black employees, only make a median wage of around $13.00 per hour.[19] If you're still not convinced that our history plays a part in today's wage inequality, look no further than tipped service workers. This European practice, which came to America in the nineteenth century, allowed restaurants, salons, railways, valets, and other service industry companies to pay below minimum wage and fill their own pockets. The discriminatory subminimum wage is ongoing in many states today.[20] Service workers, which consist predominantly of People of Color, are forced to rely on the kindness of strangers to make enough tips to feed their families. As of 2019, service employees who make more than $30 per month in tips could be legally paid as little as $2.13 per hour by their employers.[21]

The wealth gap and labor market gaps go hand in hand. In order for BIPoC families to pull themselves out of poverty, they must be able to invest in their futures. Wealth can provide education, capital to start a business, and a down payment on a house in a neighborhood with good schools, better jobs, and clean air and water. Living in neighborhoods with a healthy environment and away from industrial areas means less pollution-related health problems. Environmental illnesses can also inhibit progress in school and prevent people from working at their full capacity. Workers with college degrees are able to secure better-paying and more stable jobs. And yet, even those who are able to secure student loans to put themselves through college have another disparity hurdle to overcome. According to a report by Education Data:

■ Black and African American college graduates owe an average of $25,000 more in student loan debt than White college graduates.
■ Four years after graduation, 48 percent of Black students owe an average of 12.5 percent more than they borrowed.
■ Black and African American student borrowers are the most likely to struggle financially due to student loan debt, with 29 percent making monthly payments of $350 or more.[22]

Wealth allows families to have more options, such as relocating to take a better job with higher pay and benefits. Having less wealth means less opportunity, fewer benefits, less education, higher rates of illness, and a lower ability to handle unexpected setbacks.[23] When jobs and earnings are limited, it becomes nearly impossible to buy property or build generational wealth to pass down to children and grandchildren. Meanwhile, White families can often easily inherit real estate, valuable heirlooms, and job opportunities from their parents and grandparents. White people have had centuries to build wealth. Black, Latine, Asian, and Indigenous peoples have historically been prevented from earning and building wealth, putting them at a disadvantage, even with changing times and antidiscrimination laws. While White Americans have been getting ahead for hundreds of years, Black, Latine, and Indigenous Americans are back at the starting line trying to catch up while carrying the boulders of violence, poverty, incarceration, exclusion, profiling, and discrimination on their backs.

BUSINESS OWNERSHIP

Although the Black Codes and Jim Crow laws oppressed Black businesses, Black communities found ways to prosper. However, those Black communities that thrived through business ownership became targets of White terrorism throughout the twentieth century. Massacres, riots, and White violence destroyed Black businesses and communities. One prime example of this is the Tulsa Race Massacre. On June 1, 1921, the affluent Black community of Greenwood, also known as Black Wall Street, was looted, burned, and devastated by White rioters. As the Tulsa Historical Society and Museum describes: "35 city blocks lay in charred ruins, more than 800 people were treated for injuries and contemporary reports of deaths began at 36. Historians now believe as many as 300 people may have died."[24]

To add insult to injury, this horrific event was termed "Tulsa Race Riot" instead of being called a massacre, so insurance companies did not have to pay benefits to the people of Greenwood. This once thriving community was reduced to rubble, leaving the residents with no chance of rebuilding what was destroyed.[25]

These targeted attacks ripped wealthy Black communities apart, robbing them of financial security and stable futures. Some argue that these attacks are too far in the past to be relevant in today's society. But evidence of these stolen enterprises still exists today, in the White-owned predatory businesses that sprouted up in place of those formerly Black-owned businesses. Where community barbershops, bakeries, and flower shops once stood, there are now payday loan centers and pawnshops, shackling Black borrowers in a perpetual chain of debt.[26]

EMPLOYEE PROTECTIONS AND BENEFITS

Civil rights and antidiscrimination laws have made some progress in tipping the scales toward equality. But the progress is slow, and the movement has been marred by political and judicial setbacks. These laws have proven to work in closing wage and labor gaps. When they were strongly enforced in the 1970s, the labor market progressed toward equality. However, since the 1980s, politicians and lawmakers have essentially gutted resources from the Equal Employment Opportunity Commission (EEOC), making it much less effective.[27] At the state level, enforcement has been weak. In some states, if an employer has fewer than fifteen employees, they do not have to abide by civil rights laws, legally allowing them to discriminate against workers of Color.[28]

When it comes to employer-provided benefits, African Americans receive fewer than White employees. As of 2018, 74.8 percent of White Americans had private health insurance, while only 55.4 percent of African Americans were insured through private plans. In 2019, a study by the Employee Benefits Research Institute estimated that African American employees were 14 percent less likely to have a retirement plan through their employer than their White coworkers.[29] With a lack of health insurance and no retirement plan, the strain on Black families is significant. If the breadwinner of the family falls ill, not only will they miss work, but they will also accrue medical debt with little to no insurance. Without retirement savings, they will have to rely on family members to survive in their senior years. This can limit opportunities for younger generations to get their degrees and find stable jobs, as they will likely be paying for care or staying home to care for their elders.

According to a report by the National Immigration Law Center, people who don't have health insurance (through their employer or otherwise) are more likely to suffer from serious illness or accidents.[30] They are at an increased risk of being diagnosed with an advanced stage of a disease, or of suffering through a chronic condition that could be treated and managed with proper care and diagnosis. They are more likely to suffer permanent injury or impairment, or even die after a sudden onset condition or accident. This is due to the fact that it is common for uninsured people to delay or avoid seeking medical treatment until their condition is too serious to ignore. They typically avoid getting physicals and routine exams because they can't afford the cost. This, of course, means higher health-care costs when a health problem becomes severe due to a lack of early detection and treatment. With increased health problems, it becomes more difficult to hold down a steady job due to absences and an impaired ability to function at the job. When sick leave is not given to employees, they lose money every time they need to call out sick. Since those without benefits are more likely to become seriously ill due to ignored health warnings, they are likely to miss more work than those who are insured. This creates a perpetual cycle that is almost impossible to escape.

NONPROFITS

Racial disparity is not only evidenced in the corporate and entrepreneur worlds; it's also glaring in nonprofits across the country.
While there is some diversity in junior- and entry-level staff, a vast
majority of those in leadership roles are White. Leadership analysis
done by Battalia Winston found that "while 42% of organizations
have female executive directors, 87% of all executive directors or
presidents were white, with only minimal representation of African Americans, Asians, and Hispanic individuals."[31] For White people who come from a certain background of affluence, it's easier for
them to take lower-paying nonprofit work to build up their re-
sumes, thus snagging those executive director jobs down the road.
Other White folks may leave the nonprofit world, go and work in
the corporate world for a time, and then return to the nonprofit
world to take the leadership positions, effectively escaping middle
management and catapulting them past the lower-level staff who
have been slowly working their way up the nonprofit ladder.[32]

In a study by Echoing Green and the Bridgespan Group, racial
disparities in nonprofit leadership also spill out over fundraising
and program development, adding to the problems that many of
these nonprofits are claiming to solve.[33] For instance, Black-led
organizations in Echoing Green's Black Male Achievement Fel-
lowship brought in 45 percent less revenue than the White-led
organizations. Additionally, despite the fact that they focus on the
same work, White-led organizations enjoy 91 percent higher un-
restricted net assets than their Black-led counterparts.

I've seen firsthand that the importance of diverse boards and
program directors in nonprofits cannot be overstated. According
to the National Index of Nonprofit Board Practices, "While board
composition is not one-size-fits all, a board that is homogeneous
in any way risks having blind spots that negatively impact its

ability to make the best decisions and plans for the organization. The blind spots created by a lack of racial and ethnic diversity are particularly concerning, as they may result in strategies and plans that ineffectively address societal challenges and inequities, or even reinforce them."[34] And yet, in 2019, a survey of 102 nonprofit boards of directors revealed that 61 percent of survey respondents felt that their executive committees or boards did not accurately represent the communities they were serving.[35]

THE GOALS OF ANTIRACISM AND ANTIRACIST BUSINESS

The goal of antiracist business is to reconnect business to be in service of the people. All people. To be responsible stewards of wealth, to create jobs and opportunities that value and honor people, and to specifically contribute and lead the way forward to increasing wealth and access to opportunities, and resources that lead to equitable life outcomes among Black and Brown communities who have been marginalized and minoritized by our society and exploited by our historical business practices.

> The call for an antiracist business is a call for investment in the collective well-being of workers, consumers, entrepreneurs, and communities at large.

I often describe it as installing an elevator in your business. If you were to construct a commercial building that had multiple floors, you would need to install an elevator in that building in order to be compliant with ADA requirements. That elevator would need to meet certain standards for its location in the building, the width of the doors, and the amount of time the doors need to stay open. The intended purpose for these requirements is to provide a solution to an equity and inclusivity issue—people who can't take the stairs need a way to access the upper floors of the building. But everyone takes the elevator. The presence of an elevator in the building improves the experience of the space for everyone. We can look at the need to install an elevator as a compliance matter, or we can look at the requirement as an opportunity to create intentional space and help people feel welcome. If you've ever checked into a hotel after a long flight, with heavy luggage, only to find out that you have to walk to the other side of the building to find the elevator that will take you to your floor, you might understand how the choice we make about the elevator's location impacts how you experience the building.

This is the metaphor I use when talking about institutionalizing equitable business practices. When we take an antiracist approach to our work, create intentional space, consider and design that space for all people—especially those at the margins—establish policies and practices that center equity rather than revenue and power consolidation, the experience for everyone who interacts with that company is just better. Staff stay longer, clients and consumers become more loyal to the brand, client outcomes improve, work/life balance and self-care practices become realistic, and we become responsible stewards of wealth who reinvest and redistribute resources into other social change efforts.

Achieving this goal is going to require us to relate to one another differently. To identify the disparities between us without letting them define who we are. To accept that we all have been conditioned to prioritize White People Shit, and to acknowledge that the policies and practices that uphold racism, exploitation, colonialism, patriarchy, heteronormativity, racist capitalism, oligarchy, and so on are ours to undo and replace.

The problem, of course, is that we have this belief that business is somehow separate from our commitments to each other. The decisions that a person can make within the context of their business or leadership roles are often inconsistent with what they say they believe about justice, or other social and political issues. And this seems to be acceptable to people because, after all, it's not personal—it's business.

But as I'll soon discuss, that statement couldn't be further from the truth.

CHAPTER 3

IT'S NOT BUSINESS
IF IT'S NOT PERSONAL

When I was a graduate student trying to decide on the direction of my master's thesis, I had a mentor tell me that research was really just "me-search." She told me that her doctoral dissertation to focus on school choice in New York City had been fueled by her own experience navigating this choice as a student. As she explained, what we do in this world is always influenced by who we are. But she also confirmed the deep desire I had to change the world through the specific ways that I had confronted injustice in my own life.

> So many of us seek to change the world to fix the harms that we have personally experienced, and so many of us find ways to bring that mission into our business. Our work is often fueled by our personal experiences, context, injustices, passions, and values. And if that's not personal, I don't know what is.

So, this common phrase "It's not personal, it's business" is one of the first things we need to throw in the trash if we hope to live in a world progressing toward economic, social, and racial justice. It's a phrase most often used to justify decisions, behaviors, and actions that typically have a negative impact on a person, or a group of people, who hold less power than the decision maker (how convenient). But the fact is: business *is* deeply personal. Many entrepreneurs have stories about how their personal experiences fueled their drive to create something new, or how a mentor who took them under their wing put them on a path to success. Businesses are buzzing with interpersonal relationships that make magic happen and money flow. And the very personal decisions that an entrepreneur makes about the company they want to build can have implications on hundreds or thousands of people, and, if you're lucky enough, even the whole world.

Because of this, and because a core part of antiracist practice requires us to share our personal context and consider our own power, privilege, and position in the world, it's important that I share with you what brings me to this particular approach to business.

PERSONAL CONTEXT

As I've shared, I am a biracial, straight, cisgender, non-disabled woman. But let's get more personal than that. My father is Afro-Latino, from rural Puerto Rico. He grew up growing food and raising animals. He is a brown-skinned man who would proudly tell us that he was a descendant of Africa. My father grew up the third oldest in a family of seven children. I didn't know my grandparents well because they lived in Puerto Rico and, for various reasons, my siblings and I did not benefit from frequent visits to PR like many of my cousins and extended family. But I do know that they were proud, strict, and modest people. My father came from Puerto Rico to the mainland Estados Unidos, not speaking a word of English, and worked on farms and in factories until he joined the Army National Guard where he would serve as a full-time National Guardsman until he retired. My father was somewhat of a feminist in his own right; he would cook, clean, and take care of his kids when he wasn't working his full-time job or his part-time gig driving charter buses for extra income. Even in his retirement he still drives school buses. He taught us that how much money he made was his business, not the business of his children. He also taught us that racism was real, but that, like many forms of oppression, it was something to navigate and not give in to.

My mother is a mix of White European ethnicities, who grew up lower-class White in a low-income housing project in central Connecticut. My grandmother was the kindest person you could ever meet. She would take me "tag sale-ing" on weekends, and I would often go help her deliver the newspaper (remember those days?) and hang out with her in the summers at her job where she ran a senior center out of a converted unit in the same housing project where she lived for over thirty years—and where she raised her three daughters. My mother was the oldest. She, by her own account, was a troublemaker but also had a strong commitment to justice (in case you wondered where I got it from). She grew up with friends of all races and ethnicities and became a social justice activist and nonprofit administrator. She spoke, read, and wrote fluent Spanish. She taught us that money was bad, that standing up against injustice was good, and that if you could talk to the right person, and say the right thing, you could get all kinds of things done. I would learn later in life that there is a whole lot of White privilege, and other "-isms," wrapped up in that (more to this later).

My Titi (aunt) Kathleen, the youngest of my mom's sisters, was one of the smartest and most talented people I ever knew. She was a fighter and lived for many years with AIDS. When she found out I was pregnant when I was fifteen years old, she hugged me and told me that everything would be okay, that I was going to be an amazing mom, and not to to believe anyone who told me anything different. She didn't have any children—unless you count the dogs, cats, lizards, and squirrels that she would take in.

My Titi Celie is the caretaker in my family. She cared for my sister and me when my parents worked, and, later, my own children when I was working and at school, or just out being a twenty-something-year-old. She was born with cerebral palsy and although she often speaks of the days where she would run around the city, her disability educationally and economically marginalized her. She had one son, with one of my father's brothers.

I'm giving you this short insight into my family tree because it sets the stage for how I understand my own identity as a biracial Latina, and as a woman of Color. The fact that I only have one cousin on my maternal side, and that he is also my cousin on my paternal side, means that I don't really have an extended "White side" of the family as many other biracial people do. I had my two aunts, and my grandmother on my mother's side, and a whole bunch of aunts and uncles, and cousins and second cousins, and great-aunts and people married into the family, and so on, who were on my father's side. Culturally and ethnically, I identify as Latina. I know I am half-White. But I don't have a real context for what being White means.

Here's the thing that I often have to explain to people who want to remind me that I am "White too": when you're White, you just get to be White. I've never heard a White person tell a story about having to explain or defend their relationship with other family members because everyone is a different color or have to explain that their father doesn't need a green card and is, in fact, a United States citizen because Puerto Rico is basically a colony of the United States. I've never heard a White student share a story about being pulled over by a police officer with their parents who had been racially profiled and fearing the outcome of a routine traffic stop.

I grew up defending my identity all of the time. It's one of my most dominant memories of childhood. I certainly wasn't White enough to pass as a "full-White," as my friend Elizabeth DiAlto calls it. Peers, and sometimes adults, often didn't believe my father was my father, or my cousins were my cousins, because of the differences in our complexions. Genetics has no rhyme or reason when it comes to skin tone and mixed families. Even among siblings who share two biological parents, it's not uncommon to have a variety of complexions, hair textures, and features distributed among the kids.

So, this was my early personal context. My parents, who worked hard but didn't make a lot of money, got divorced when I was ten. Soon after, we lost the nine-hundred-square-foot home my parents purchased when I was three because my mother couldn't afford to keep it, and I never truly felt at home anywhere again until I became a homeowner in the fall of 2020.

FURTHER INTO THE MARGINS

In grad school, I remember downloading Excel files from the Department of Public Health Vital Records division. I wanted to see the primary source data on birth rates in Connecticut for the years between 1997 and 2010. At the time, I was studying and working in the field of teen pregnancy prevention and young parent support. I wanted to understand how teen pregnancy rates changed between the time I was a teen mom, to the time I was working with teen parents. I wanted to know if all the money being pumped into teen pregnancy prevention programs into the inner city and rural White communities was working. I wanted to understand what made some programs more effective than others, and how we even defined efficacy.

In 1997, there were eighty-three babies born to teenage mothers fifteen years old and younger in the state of Connecticut, twenty-six of which were living in Hartford County. And as I looked over that data, I had somewhat of an out-of-body experience. I realized that one of those numbers in that Excel sheet was me. There I was. An actual statistic. And it made me angry. Because that number didn't communicate any story of mine, or my peers who also became young mothers around the same time. It only communicated a number that would be grouped together by other researchers like me, looking at this data, and would link this data with other statistics that said that many of us would have a hard time graduating high school and holding living-wage jobs. That we would experience extreme poverty for extended periods of time, and possibly forever. That our sons would drop out of high school and be involved with law enforcement before they turned eighteen, and that our daughters would also be teen moms continuing the cycle of poverty and teen parenthood. Those researchers might have encountered the statistic that only 1 percent of that population would get a bachelor's degree before they turned thirty. And although I was proud that I had done that, it bothered me that I was the 1 percent, even though my odds were far worse because, according to the data, with every subsequent birth a teen mom had, the odds would double against her. And shortly after I gave birth to my son in April 1997, I got pregnant again.

When you're sixteen years old with two children and trying to get on and off of public transportation by yourself, the world has some pretty strong messages it wants to tell you. None of them are good. I remember strangers asking me if my children had the same father, asking me how old I was, and what my life plan was going to be. They'd tell me I'd be a burden, and how their tax money was going to have to support me for the rest of my life. And these weren't just whispers and side-eye glances. These were the explicit words that came out of people's mouths. From social workers, teachers, strangers at the bank. And yes, these were all White folks. There seemed to be a disgust about my situation, and a degree of audacity and entitlement that allowed these people to say the meanest things to me. Even though, in some cases, these were adults who were supposed to care about me. I vividly remember walking out of the school building midday, seven months pregnant and knowing deep inside of me that I would never be back. I dropped out of school in ninth grade, and no one cared. I was allowed to just disappear.

A chance connection changed everything for me. I enrolled in a program for parenting teens that was led by a woman who would show me how impactful coaching could be. She would have never called herself a coach, but she was one of the most naturally skilled coaches I ever met. She didn't treat us like teen moms, but she treated us like teenagers who needed to get their shit together, graduate high school, go to college, and figure out what they were going to do with their lives. During my time in that program, I would get my GED, start and finish my associate's degree, and continue on to pursue a bachelor's in theater. Shortly after graduating from college, I became the program manager of that very same teen mom program and would start my master's degree in psychology, specializing in public administration and social change. I had a successful career in the nonprofit sector because of my unique combination of life experiences and academic achievements, but it didn't take long for me to realize that I was not going to see the financial return on investment of my education. I was still qualifying for food stamps even while working full-time with a college degree.

I was ambitious, smart, and tired of being broke. It was around this time that I met my future husband, who saw something in me that I couldn't see and encouraged me to start a consulting side-hustle. He taught me some of the basics of negotiating a work agreement, making sure I got paid on time, and being more confident in sharing my story because it was, ironically, also a unique sales proposition. I became a full-time nonprofit professional by day, and youth development and diversity, equity, and inclusion consultant by evening/nights/weekends and vacation days, and sometimes lunch breaks.

Now that you understand this, maybe you see why the super trendy online business advice I was getting about packing up your life, starting a blog, and borrowing money to start your own business was not going to work for me. You might also understand why I deeply believe that business is most definitely personal.

Because not only do our personal experiences drive our desire for change; our businesses grow because of relationships between people. Business dealings are done through handshakes and over dinners where people talk about their children, hobbies, and partners. Even corporate cultures that want to discourage politics and personal connection between their employees engage in relationship-building at exclusive country clubs and over expensive dinners. Friend and family rates, legacy preferences, and recurring client incentives are all meant to honor personal relationships. Business is only "not personal" when someone makes a decision that is in their own best interests and when their decisions are rooted in things like capitalism, exploitation, oppression, colonialism, or systemic racism.

> Because, honestly, it's not business if it's not personal.

Impersonalization is akin to dehumanization. Impersonalizing business allows us to act without deeply considering the lasting impacts of our choices. It allows us to make choices that are in "the company's" best interests instead of searching for options that are in the best interests of the collective. It allows us to make decisions that consolidate power and resources rather than distributing it, even when there is already more than enough at the top. "It's not personal, it's business" is the very ideology that led so many corporations during the COVID-19 pandemic to lay off their employees and file for bankruptcy while paying out hundreds of millions of dollars in salaries and bonuses to CEOs, executives, and shareholders. Frankly, these decisions are unacceptable.

MAKING IT PERSONAL

The first step in becoming an antiracist entrepreneur is to bring the personal back into business. A critical component of any antiracist practice is connection, community, and the willingness to share power. We can't do any of those things without being willing to be personal. Before you get any ideas in your head about improving your company culture by rolling out more company retreats and "icebreaker" activities in an effort to get to know your team better, let me be clear: that is not what we're talking about here. Antiracist practice is not interested in performative activities designed to turn coworkers into friends or, worse, "family."

In fact, your "family-like" atmosphere is probably doing more harm than good. This isn't an effort to make people feel better about their workplace by introducing "fun" as the secret sauce of workplace culture.

> Antiracist practice asks us to disrupt, dismantle, and destroy the policies and practices that perpetuate the status quo, the systems that contribute to oppression and exploitation, and any and all practices rooted in White supremacy.

Company retreats, client events, employee recognition, and more fun are not going to do the job of re-personalizing company cultures in ways that support antiracist practices because these things are mostly symbolic gestures that allow corporate executives, and managers, owners, and other leaders, to appear available, accessible, and down to earth. They're also used as ways to build morale or pump people up about returning to work to do it all again. And oftentimes, these efforts fall flat or become performative actions that are fundamentally meaningless but that give the appearance that the company is taking action or trying to make progress. Take the example of the Amazon warehouse workers in Chicago who took to social media to share their disgust by Amazon's gesture to recognize Juneteenth, a newly designated federal holiday, with a celebration of Black culture and Black businesses by serving fried chicken and waffles for lunch rather than giving workers a paid day off, or increased holiday pay, or something that would actually create equity, like, I don't know . . . paying a living wage, for example. Nope. Instead of real systemic change that would not only celebrate the contributions of Black people but also help to fix a broken system, warehouse workers got chicken and waffles. Elsewhere within Amazon's corporate structure, Jeff Bezos sent a memo to all employees that read:[1]

Subject: Juneteenth

Over the past few weeks, the Steam and I have spent a lot of time listening to customers and employees and thinking about how recent events in our country have laid bare the systemic racism and injustices that oppress Black individuals and communities.

This Friday, June 19, is Juneteenth, the oldest-known celebration commemorating the end of slavery in the U.S.

I'm canceling all of my meetings on Friday, and I
encourage all of you to do the same if you can. We're
providing a range of online learning opportunities for
employees throughout the day.

Please take some time to reflect, learn, and support each
other. Slavery ended a long time ago, but racism didn't.

Jeff

There are a few things that are very interesting about this
memo that reflect the very depersonalization that I am referring
to. First of all, in his very first sentence, Bezos says that he and his
"Steam" (the internal name for his executive leadership team) are
spending time talking to people about recent events that have
"laid bare the systemic racism and injustices that oppress Black
individuals and communities." But he did not say whether they
were looking at how Amazon itself is replicating these injustices
through its workplace policies, practices, and spaces. A relational,
personalized conversation that centered the needs of the most
marginalized members of the community would not focus on the
situations of the external events in the country, but rather on the
internal environment of the institution itself. Just weeks before
this memo was released, Amazon had to close construction on a
warehouse site in central Connecticut after the FBI launched an
investigation because workers found eight nooses at the site over
the course of a month. By focusing conversations on what's happening in the world around us, rather than naming the ways that
our own institutions replicate, facilitate, or become the environments where injustice occurs, we are attempting to create distance between ourselves and our responsibility.

Aside from the deflection from how Amazon itself replicates
oppression, the second part of the memo only applies to a small
and disparate group of workers who have agency over their own

schedules. Do you think that the day-to-day warehouse workers have meetings they can opt out of? Can you imagine a delivery driver pulling over in a parking lot to engage in online learning instead of delivering that package that someone is sitting at their window waiting for?

This memo was not written to the underpaid laborers who make up the majority of Amazon's workforce. Bezos was not thinking about them or a more equitable way to commemorate the day that should stand for justice, freedom, equitable labor, and reparations for the most marginalized individuals. And I can tell you, making reparations does not include providing a free meal that reinforces stereotypes, and they most definitely aren't made through giving people with white-collar jobs a day off from meetings.

So, although your company softball tournament might be fun, it's not an activity that will fundamentally change the nature of our relationships that will lead to policy changes and more equity in the workplace. The performative gestures don't create opportunities to have conversations about the impact of the constant retraumatization from our news cycle and how it might impact people's ability to concentrate at work. They don't provide opportunities for parents to name their fear of sending their children to school in the middle of a pandemic. They don't address the need to facilitate dialogues between supervisors and staff members who are being held to standards that, although may seem appropriate in a physical office, are not suitable for remote-work environments.

Moving away from activities that foster morale and team-building and moving toward actual antiracist business practices means that we are creating new policies, new procedures, and new practices that provide the structure for keeping things personal and minimizing harm by requiring us to take accountability when we fail. We need policies and practices that allow us to institutionalize a culture of interpersonalization and to value the humanity and needs of all workers.

I also don't want you to think that this is only relevant for big business. Even if you are a solopreneur, building your own website at your kitchen table in between serving clients or shipping products, you can build policies, procedures, and practices that cultivate connection with your clients, customers, vendors, contactors, and broader community while setting a strong, antiracist foundation for your future. Start as you mean to go on.

CULTURE CHANGE

The shift to personalizing business is really a matter of culture change. Culture change is not easy, but it's also not impossible. Shifting your culture requires you to understand what makes up a culture in the first place. Without getting too far down the cultural psychology rabbit hole, culture emerges in any place where there is prolonged interaction between humans. Many social scientists describe different factors, including our ecological environment, our social environment, and our biology. Features of culture include all of the elements we identify as belonging to a specific group or subgroups, including language and dialects of language, ideologies, religions, traditions, foods, dress, behaviors, and norms. And as ideologies, beliefs, and ecological and biological conditions shift, our culture shifts too. In 2020, we all experienced a unique moment in our cultural histories, in which most of us adapted to simultaneous disruptions in our ecological, social, and biological environments, and our culture has changed as a result of these disruptions. In 2019, in the United States, a large group of people wearing masks on a street would be cause for alarm. Today, we accept that mask-wearing is a choice and realize that the individual wearing the mask could be sick, unvaccinated, or a member of a high-risk class. Or it could just be a personal choice. Either way, our culture has adapted to mask-wearing. At this very moment, there is a huge pushback in workplace culture where employees are refusing to return to the office; the extended period of time during which many people have been working from home has changed the culture of work. It has shaped an understanding that working from home is sometimes more productive than being in an office, and much less stressful than being subject to office politics, personalities, and daily microaggressions. Our culture is shaped by our environment, and you, as a leader in business, have control over the environment you create for your teams and your customers.

RE-PERSONALIZING YOUR BUSINESS

Let's get in there and do some work. How can you create a culture that values interpersonal relationships? A culture that values the humanity of your employees? Will you acknowledge your own identities? Where do you hold power and privilege? Are you using that power and privilege responsibly and justly, and creating practices and policies that create connection and shared accountability?

Here are five things you can do to re-personalize your business:

1. **When you need to make a decision about a policy, procedure, or major shift in business, talk to the people who would be most impacted by that decision.** This will help you stay connected to the real-life, daily implications of your own decision making. Also, the people most impacted by the decision often have insight about processes and side effects of your choice that you just may not be aware of because you're not looking at it from their vantage point.

2. **Use check-in questions to start meetings with team members, clients, or collaborators.** Check-in questions,

icebreakers, or just making time to prioritize listening to how everyone's weekends went are ways to connect people. It's during these times that we learn things about our teams that we may not have known before; we get to know about their families, hobbies, dreams, and so on. The desire to get right down to business and skip the chitchat creates an often unnecessary urgency that causes anxiety and can leave people feeling disconnected and isolated.

3. **Examine your own identity and privilege.** When we take the time to unpack our own identities and privilege, we become more aware and sensitive to how other people's identities are determining factors in their own lives. We become better advocates for the movement for racial justice and can become models of how to sit in uncomfortable conversations that will move communities forward when things get difficult.

4. **If you have to make a decision that will have a negative impact on someone, consider the ways to minimize harm.** Being a leader or executive sometimes comes with the responsibility to make difficult decisions that will have negative consequences on others' lives. We may have to lay people off, or disengage from employment because of performance or other issues. We may have to change the course of the direction for a company that may impact the work that people are doing. Either way, when we are clear about how choices impact others, we can minimize harm by being communicative and open, as well as giving people time to adjust. We can support people with additional training or coaching. If we have to let people go, we can do so in ways that are values-driven by giving them advanced notice (if appropriate), paying

severance packages, offering to write letters of recommendation, or providing other job placement support.

5. **Reprioritize humans, not just the human capital.** When we think of humans as capital, we are overemphasizing the elements of our life that are about production, productivity, and expertise because they can be converted into a monetary value. When we prioritize the human, we take a holistic approach to management and consider things like self-care, health, time with family and community, personal growth, and interests. We realize that when people can nurture all parts of themselves, they become more effective collaborators and are likely to stay with a company longer.

Business is personal, and the more we are able to identify and integrate this idea into our business practices, the more we are able to honor our full humanity, amplifying strengths and creating opportunities for growth. This is equity. It's not just about the standardization of practices; it's about honoring the individual as a critical component of the collective.

CHAPTER 4

FROM TOXIC CAPITALISM TO JUST COMMERCE

'll never forget a conversation I had in my mid-twenties with a friend. She was about ten years older than me, but because I had been such a young mother we had kids in the same age group. She was one of the few people who could relate to some of the motherhood dilemmas I was facing. I remember sitting at her kitchen table as she explained her frustration over her employment situation. She had been offered a promotion that would have come with a small raise from $11.00 to $15.00. Although this might seem like a cause for celebration, it wasn't. What she had figured out was that this potential promotion was not going to provide her enough of an income increase to make up for the difference between what she'd lose in social aid benefits. Accepting the promotion would actually cause her to become more financially stressed than she already was. She would lose her food stamp benefits, and her rent would increase because her housing subsidy would decrease. In addition, although her children would be covered, she would lose her eligibility for free health care, which meant that she would have to purchase it from her employer. The four-dollar-an-hour increase in wages would result in a loss of overall household income for her family. So, she didn't accept the promotion.

I remember being faced with a similar choice just a year later. The ceiling in my apartment collapsed and I started to look for other apartments. I was also a recipient of Section 8, a federal housing subsidy that makes apartment-hunting particularly stressful. Despite laws against discrimination of families with Section 8, landlords and property management companies can be creative about how to keep recipients out. It's supposed to be illegal to even ask a potential tenant if they have a housing sub- sidy, but when I was a young parent looking for low-rent apart- ments, I was always asked. Some landlords will straight up tell you they don't accept housing subsidies; others will say they only will rent to people who have them because at least the rent is guaranteed. One way of keeping people out is to price apart- ments way out of the rental limits for Section 8, although once in a while you'll encounter a landlord who is willing to take your housing subsidy if you'll pay them cash under the table to make up the difference.

By the time my ceiling caved in, I was done dealing with grimy landlords, and I had been lucky enough to recently get a job work- ing full-time at an art gallery facilitating educational program- ming about social justice movements. I was making $35,000 a year (which is about $673 dollars a week before taxes) and was a super confident twenty-six-year-old. I believed the story I'd been told. I got my degree, I got a job, and I was ready to collect on the promise of upward mobility, if not stability. So I gave up my hous- ing voucher so that I could get an apartment I wanted. A year and a half later I found myself in a work environment that was toxic, misogynistic, and racist. I was depressed, and the thought of re- turning to work after the birth of my third child was unbearable.

I wasn't able to find a new job fast enough and soon we were facing an eviction.

I share these two stories to give you a sense of the choices that people are making between working and living, maintaining their physical and mental health and their personal dignity. Families at this level of economic insecurity are taking a gamble when they choose between caring for children and just scraping by, or taking an opportunity that might give them a better quality of life in the long run, but requires them to give up their safety net in the short term. My friend wasn't willing to take the risk. She kept her housing subsidy, her food stamp benefits, and health care, and when she ultimately had to leave the job because she could no longer work her third-shift hours because of day care, there was no major crisis. When I left my job, my three kids, my partner, and I had to temporarily move in with family and regroup.

> Living-wage jobs with mandatory minimum wages that take people above the poverty line; job security and unions; healthy workplace policies and cultures; and policies like universal basic income and universal health care—all of these things would have real impact on the ways people live and work.

According to conservative political ideology, these are radical anti-capitalist ideas that will stifle our economy and ultimately negatively impact business. But what these changes would actually do is disrupt what I call "toxic capitalism," moving us toward antiracist policies and practices, create more equity, and shift the power of the ruling class.

Oxford dictionary defines "capitalism" as "an economic and political system in which a country's trade and industry are controlled by private owners for profit, rather than by the state." Although this is an oversimplified definition for what capitalism actually means in practice, the idea that capitalism is merely private ownership of business for profit makes the concept seem very innocent and easily defendable by reasonable people. Capitalism is much more sinister in practice.

In his book *How to Be an Antiracist*, Ibram X. Kendi uses the term "racial capitalism" and describes how capitalism and racism are conjoined twins. There is really no way to separate how the labor of enslaved Africans and Indigenous peoples throughout the Americas, Caribbean Islands, and South Pacific directly fueled our global economy and the ways in which this has affected the wealth creation and consolidation of the White ruling class that persists today. Even after slavery was abolished, there was no policy enforcement for reparations that could have served to create more equitable outcomes for those who were freed, and there were no policy standards for compensation that could have prevented the oppressive and exploitative conditions that free people experienced as sharecroppers and laborers after the gradual abolishment of slavery throughout the United States.

It was supremacist ideologies that allowed White colonizers to enslave people for commercial gain. White people considered themselves better, smarter, more beautiful; they believed they practiced the "right" religion, spoke the "right" languages, and were more civilized than the people they encountered when they showed up to a land to which they were not invited. They decided that they were more worthy and that the people they found were less human, enabling them to overtake the people and the land.

These same supremacist ideologies persist today and continue to uphold racial capitalism. Only now the supremacist ideology has become so institutionalized that even people who don't believe they are inherently better than someone else participate in a system that holds them in higher regard, allowing them to become actors in the oppression of others just by doing what their job or position requires of them.

Let's take Foot Locker, for example. In 2020, like most retailers, Foot Locker, a major American retailer of athletic shoes and clothing, closed its stores and furloughed its in-store workers because of the economic effects of the global coronavirus pandemic, which resulted in shutdowns of most in-person shopping for most of the United States and abroad.[1] Although Foot Locker's job postings don't include salaries, self-reports from Foot Locker employees share that they make minimum wage to a few dollars above, depending on the position. Executives of the company made the choice to furlough workers because stores were not open, and therefore the company could not make their revenue goals in order to pay their employees. This seems like a logical, rational decision, albeit a tragic one.

However, this logic didn't seem to apply to executives in the company. In 2020, even though the company did not meet its financial goals for the year, and technically, according to its own policy, CEO Richard Johnson did not meet the requirements for his 2020 bonus, the board decided to calculate an adjustment (basically, pretend money) that Foot Locker would have made if the company were operating under normal conditions, and then lowered the minimum revenue goal that would qualify executives for bonuses, which ultimately resulted in Johnson earning a $3.8 million cash bonus in addition to his $8+ million salary. He made more money in 2020 than he did in 2019.

> This is capitalism. It protects and provides for the people at the top, unfettered by government oversight or regulation, and further marginalizes and oppresses people at the bottom.

Why don't we all stand up and break down this clearly unfair system? The only reason I can think of is supremacist ideology. Because in order to justify these kinds of choices, one must accept that the people at the top are inherently better, smarter, and more worthy of protection and accommodation even though they don't need it. Even though there are others who need it so badly that their basic needs can't be met.

It's situations like these that leave people with a negative outlook when it comes to our economic system and create a narrative that encourages more socially conscious leaders to opt out of entrepreneurship altogether. One of the biggest moral dilemmas that a lot of my clients describe to me is their lack of desire to participate in capitalism, which impacts their ability to charge for their services and make the transition from a side-hustler to a business owner. Some of them believe that capitalism is morally wrong, others come from backgrounds in nonprofit work or education and have really jacked up relationships with making money, and yet others have been so burned out by business and hustle culture that they become fearful of reproducing it. Here's the thing: You can open up a day care center out of your home, set your own fees, and own your business—that's capitalism. A college student can start an online T-shirt business between classes and support themselves   that's capitalism. The problem is that the ability for major retailers to lay off thousands of workers while paying out millions of dollars to executives and shareholders is also capitalism.

Defenders of capitalism and trickle-down economics would argue that capitalism cultivates innovation, progress, solutions, and free markets. What they believe is that consumer demand breeds healthy competition to make better products, which in turn keeps prices in check and keeps business operating with integrity. This is the version of capitalism grounded in the work of Scottish philosopher Adam Smith. His thinking proposed that people will always act in their best interests, and that this in turn would keep the economy in check because if someone was acting in a way that was not part of the social good, others would no longer support them. He describes this concept in his book *Theory of Moral Sentiments* (1759) as the "invisible hand":

> They are led by an **invisible hand** to make nearly the same distribution of the necessaries of life, which would have been made, had the earth been divided into equal portions among all its inhabitants, and thus without intending it, without knowing it, advance the interest of the society, and afford means to the multiplication of the species.[2]

Smith believed that the owning class would be responsible stewards of their wealth—not because of some spiritual connection or moral responsibility, but because it was in the owner's best interests to distribute wages and benefits to the laborers that were essential to the owner's ability to maintain their land, home, and business ventures.

According to Smith's vision of capitalism, businesses should behave in the best interests of their consumers and workers because it's ultimately in their own best interests. The theoretical checks and balances are the consumers themselves, who would always have the option to shop elsewhere if a company were acting in its own self interests. This type of self-regulating utopian economy would need little governmental regulation.

What Smith wasn't able to foresee in the late 1700s was a system in which there is such extreme ownership and wealth that consumers' choices are so limited, and workers' options equally bleak, that businesses can act in their best interests even when their interests are in direct conflict with what's in the best interests of consumers, the environment, and even the physical health and safety of their workers.

Over the last couple of years, as I've been trying to detangle capitalism from economics, commerce, business, income, and justice, what I realize is that what capitalism actually means (or, more accurately, what it could mean) really depends on who you ask and what kind of spin they want to put on the word in order to make it more palatable. The following section provides some current definitions and approaches to capitalism.

OLIGARCHIC CAPITALISM

An oligarchy is a government that's run by a few corrupt, privileged people, usually formed by a despotic power.[3] But here's the real secret of an oligarchy: it usually disguises itself as a democracy. America is increasingly being run by the wealthiest people in the country, which actually makes it a plutocracy. When a government is influenced by the few wealthiest people in the country, it tends to only work in favor of that particular class of people. America's billionaires are using their money and power to influence politics, avoid paying taxes, and ensure they keep getting richer on the backs of the majority of the citizens, who are not billionaires. In 2021, the ten wealthiest American billionaires consisted of nine White men and one White woman.[4] When the top wealthiest White people influence policy, anyone who is not White and wealthy gets left out of the equation.

In her book *How the South Won the Civil War*, historian Heather Cox Richardson claims that the nation is gripped in a moral struggle between oligarchy and democracy.[5] She believes an oligarchic America began with the ideals of slaveholders, and that vision came to be in the second half of the twentieth century, with movement conservatism.[6] This new oligarchy is fueled by racism and economic domination by the wealthy and elite. It started with Barry Goldwater, then grew more powerful through the Nixon, Reagan, and Bush administrations, and eventually led to the pinnacle of racism and corruption with the Trump presidency. Modern conservatives are now doing the bidding of the Confederacy, rolling back the progress of the New Deal and arguing that any fair tax on the rich is just a ploy to redistribute wealth from the top wealthiest White men and give it to BIPoC and women. Many of these rich White men are funding a campaign to destroy democracy in favor of oligarchic capitalism, which only furthers the agenda of White supremacy in this country.

STATE-GUIDED CAPITALISM

In state-guided capitalism, the economy is controlled by the state, which uses the markets for political gains, such as in China, Russia, and Venezuela.[7] Friendlier examples are Norway, New Zealand, and Sweden. In free-market economies, such as those in the United States, Japan, and Europe, corporations drive the economy. State-controlled economies can control major resources, such as the oil industry—75 percent of which is controlled by government-owned companies in places like Saudi Arabia and Norway. This makes it difficult for free-market companies to compete in the countries in which state-controlled companies are the primary competition. In China, for instance, the United States is competing with the state-enmeshed auto industry, making it hard to maintain an advantage. Google made the decision to move their operations out of China because of strict government censorship, not to mention the fact that their intellectual property had been stolen due to the government playing by their own rules rather than those of the free market.[8]

CONSCIOUS CAPITALISM

Conscious capitalism is touted as an approach to capitalism that is more ethical, encouraging founders to connect to a higher purpose of the vision. John Mackey and Raj Sisodia have described a version of capitalism that holds the possibility of creating "multiple kinds of value and wellbeing for all stakeholders: financial, intellectual, physical, ecological, social, cultural, emotional, ethical, and even spiritual."[9] Mackey, who was the CEO of Whole Foods, spearheaded this movement, and for a long time Whole Foods worked to live out the values of conscious capitalism by offering health care to part-time employees and profit-sharing initiatives. Mackey believed that if more people practiced conscious capitalism, consumers would respond by spending their dollars with these conscious companies, thereby putting pressure on the market to respond with more companies practicing conscious capitalism. Mackey didn't believe in labor unions, or governmental regulation, and essentially believed that everyone in the system would do the right thing.

Ironically, in 2017, Amazon, arguably one of the most controversial companies, acquired Whole Foods and shortly after cut initiatives including profit sharing and health benefits to part-time employees. John Mackey stayed on as CEO of Whole Foods. Under his leadership, during the COVID-19 pandemic some employees were asked to remove face masks with Black Lives Matter printed on them. They were told to either wear a blank face mask provided by the store or be sent home without pay. Mackey's argument for this was that the store has a policy about employee uniforms in which the staff is not allowed to wear clothing featuring any logos, religious statements, or causes.[10]

According to the *New York Times*, although Amazon published a statement in support of the "fight against systemic racism," CEO Jeff Bezos and other company executives, including Jay Carney, a former press secretary for the Obama administration, planned to unleash a smear campaign against a Black employee.[11] They sent out a company memo outlining an attempt to discredit a Black employee who was fired after leading a warehouse walkout for unsafe working conditions during the COVID-19 pandemic. They called Christopher Smalls, the employee who led the walkout, "not smart or articulate." Amazon General Counsel David Zapolsky took notes at the executive meeting that read, "We should spend the first part of our response strongly laying out the case for why the organizer's conduct was immoral, unacceptable, and arguably illegal, in detail, and only then follow with our usual talking points about worker safety. Make him the most interesting part of the story, and if possible make him the face of the entire union/organizing movement."[12] In other words, the executives planned to use this Black organizer as a way to discredit the entire labor movement at Amazon.

So-called conscious capitalism demonstrates a desire to believe that people are inherently good and inherently motivated by the best interests of the collective, but it does not demonstrate a real desire for accountability and systemic change.

HUMAN CAPITALISM

Andrew Yang, former presidential candidate and entrepreneur, makes a compelling argument for a human-centered approach to a capitalist system organized on three key tenets. 1) Humanity is more important than money. 2) The unit of an economy is each person, not each dollar. 3) Markets exist to serve our common goals and values.[13]

His proposed "human capitalism" would combine holistic metrics for business success—such as environmental progress, human quality of life index, health, and other factors—in addition to financial metrics, with policy solutions including mandatory minimum wage, Medicare for all, and universal basic income. These initiatives are considered anti-capitalist because they would create more governmental oversight, and some argue that they would stifle innovation and job creation as companies would be required to pay more in taxes.

But none of these variations on capitalism address the fundamental problem of racial disparities, or even wealth disparities, in our overall population. Currently, there is no version of capitalism, or any other economic system for that matter, that demonstrates the ability to combat racism or any form of social disparities. Canada and most of Europe utilize capitalism as an economic system while maintaining social safety-net programs, supplying free health care and extended maternity leave, and providing access to free public higher education—all policies considered anti-capitalist by conservatives—yet somehow we still consider these nations capitalistic.

We can dislike capitalism as much as we want, but there's still not another economic system in the modern world that has successfully demonstrated an ability to efficiently care for its people's health, education, quality of life, housing, and other social needs, and is devoid of racial disparities. So perhaps it's time for some magical thinking, or maybe manifesting, where we get to imagine a different option, pulling from some of the best ideas and applying a lens for justice, equity, and antiracism.

JUST COMMERCE

What I propose to my clients—and to those of you who still feel the desire to distance yourself from all of the elements of capitalism that are toxic, oppressive, exploitative, and racist—is an orientation to business that moves us toward "just commerce." Commerce in itself is simply the exchange of goods and services, which people do every day in a multitude of scenarios. Commerce is purchasing a home; it is purchasing candy from the candy house (if you were fortunate enough to grow up in a neighborhood with a candy house); it's also trading babysitting hours with another member of your community. Therefore, just commerce is an approach to the exchange of goods and services that pursues justice as a measure of success in its practice. Just commerce centers the goals of antiracism and aims to be the kind of economic model that repairs our own relationship to toxic capitalism, so that more of us can participate in business ownership and wealth building while releasing the psychological, emotional, and practical connections that capitalism leaves behind.

Just commerce can be thought of as an approach to a small business model or an overall economic system. As a model for small businesses, the emphasis is on creating a viable living wage for owners; creating jobs for others if needed; offering benefits as soon as the company is able to; having paid time off, reasonable workloads, equity-centered hiring plans (more on this in Chapter 10); and reinvesting time and money into the community.

As an example of how this works at a small business or for solo-entrepreneur businesses, let's look at a conversation I had with a private client I worked with a number of years back. On one of our first calls, when I asked her what she wanted her work to look like, she said, "I want to work forty hours a week, but I want ten of those hours to go toward my volunteer advocacy work for undocumented residents." We then came up with a business model that allowed her to work thirty hours a week in her businesses: fifteen in billable hours, fifteen in business development time, allowing her to allocate ten hours toward her impact work. This meant her rates needed to be higher in order for her to meet her revenue goals, and she needed clear, intentional strategies for marketing and outreach to attract these clients who would not only pay new rates but also do so happily because they shared the values of liberation, justice, and the rights of undocumented people.

Although the rates were higher than she was originally comfortable with, she was able to see how engaging in this type of commerce and charging her new rates would enable her to impact justice efforts in her community, while still having time to spend with her family and friends without burning out from overworking.

As an overall economic system, I imagine that just commerce would measure our individual and collective economic health by considering a number of factors, including:

- Racial disparities at all earning levels;
- Representation among leadership of large and small businesses;
- Representation of board and shareholders;
- Mandatory minimum wages, eliminating the need for people to work more than one job to cover their basic necessities;
- An expanded definition of basic needs that includes the ability for people to have savings for things like purchasing homes, traveling, or engaging in other personal development activities;
- Universal basic income;
- Medicare for all so that people's access to health care is permanently disconnected from their employment status;
- Expanded definitions of unemployment, underemployment, and homelessness, with accurate reporting of this data;
- Equitable taxes on the top income earners and corporations;
- Elimination of private prisons, juvenile detention centers, and reform of cash-bonding practices;
- Elimination or significant reform and oversight of payday loan practices;

- Reform of school funding so that all schools, no matter their location, have equitable access to high-quality education initiatives and necessary resources;
- Extended mandatory paid leave supported by government initiatives; and
- Robust social-impact business initiatives that go beyond corporate responsibility and sponsorship.

Just commerce isn't simply an offhanded notion. It is a new guide to doing business. It offers us a new economic system that we can create and re-create within the old one. As much as the radical in me wants to "tear it down," when has that process actually been successful? When has it ever happened without terrible bloodshed and trauma?

> We don't need to risk ourselves to change the system. We just have to build a new system while we're divesting from the old one.

We create a new order of business even as the old one begins to collapse. Time is in our favor, but only if we are willing to take action. In order to create just commerce, we have to be willing to renegotiate the old ways—even ones that may have benefited us. Because as long as our choices are benefiting a system of oppression, racism, and inequity, we are supporting the oppressors. There is a way toward liberation that also increases profit. When I worked in nonprofits, it never seemed fair that people who were curing diseases were supposed to be poor (limiting access to those jobs) while the people causing them were lauded for being wealthy. We can do good work and be rewarded for it. We can create antiracist businesses and still be competitive. We can reject the tenets of toxic capitalism and still accumulate wealth.

We don't need to sacrifice our own goals, dreams, and comforts in order to also be just, equitable, and antiracist. We can practice just commerce in our businesses, and we can create a new world in which wealth and justice work together.

PART 2

BUILDING YOUR ANTIRACIST BUSINESS

Money is like water. Water can be a precious life-giving resource. But what happens when water is dammed, when a water cannon is fired on protestors in subzero temperatures? Money should be a tool of love, to facilitate relationships, to help us thrive, rather than to hurt and divide us. If it's used for sacred, life-giving, restorative purposes, it can be medicine.

EDGAR VILLANUEVA

CHAPTER 5

START WITH YOUR VALUES

I spent years working with nonprofits and facilitating workshops to help varied organizations come up with their core values, mission statements, and vision statements. Sometimes it would take several sessions for the group to come to an agreement on a statement, only to get negative feedback from others and cause them to second-guess all their work and start again. The ironic part was that these mission statements and values exercises didn't really matter. There were just words to be put on grant applications, websites, and on decorative plaques to be hung in the hallways on office buildings. They were concepts. Ideals. But all too often the work stopped there.

The first step in building an antiracist business, or moving toward antiracism in your current business, is to determine the soul of your work, which goes beyond a mission and vision statement. I think of it as the fundamental beliefs that your business holds that influence every single aspect of its operations. We discover these beliefs by identifying five core values and becoming clear on your commitments. These two things, along with your impact purpose (which we'll cover in Chapter 6), make up the DNA of your anti-racist business and will inspire all of the decisions that you make moving forward. For businesses that have been around for a while and are moving in the direction of antiracism, this values work will drive your growth plan. It will become your compass to pull you out of default practices that are rooted in toxic capitalism, corporate culture, and individualism, and ultimately move you toward a liberated company with an active antiracist praxis.

VALUES ARE A TOOL

When I help clients work on business planning, the very first thing we do, no matter where they are in their business journey, is identify the core values of the entrepreneur or leadership team. These values become the touchstone for all the work and the decisions made on behalf of the whole business. Again, it isn't about a mission statement on the wall—this is what guides every decision, choice, and action made on part of the business. Sometimes, clients will tell me that they've already identified their core values. They've had another consultant walk them through a values process, or they read a book and came up with them on their own; in most of these cases, however, the values that they've come up with are a list of things that they believe their business *should* value, instead of what the entrepreneur or team actually believe are the most important things. And nine times out of ten, during our values session they realize that the values they started with are not aligned with what they want to build.

Our values should represent the things that we believe in as people (remember, it's not business if it's not personal) and as stewards of our business, not the things we think the business *should* value separate from ourselves. When we approach values work from this external perspective, we place the business outside of ourselves and make it something that exists without a human connection. We depersonalize it, which makes it easy for us to come up with values that sound great but are not useful in our day-to-day decision making, and quickly become disconnected from the people that the business is designed to serve.

> Our values have the potential to be powerful business tools if we let them, but we need to be clear on what they are and what they mean, making sure that we are not valuing something that is in direct conflict with antiracist principles.

WHAT VALUES ARE

Values will obviously vary from person to person. My suggestion is to have five. This doesn't mean that you don't have other values, but by selecting five core values you are drawing a line in the sand about where you stand and what's most important. I would argue that once you go beyond five, you lose the ability to use the word "core" since core means the things that are most central. The more values you have, the less useful they become in your day-to-day practice.

Here is a quick exercise that you can use to help you identify your core values:

1. Take out a sheet of paper or open up a document on your computer.
2. Set a timer for one minute.
3. Write down a list of the values that are most important to you. I suggest you let them be words that represent bigger ideas. For example: justice, love, beauty, simplicity. If

you're getting stuck with what your values are, think about the things that tend to fire you up or excite you, as well as the things you rally behind or are in pursuit of.

4. Stop writing when your timer goes off, or once you've written down ten to twelve words.

5. Step away from the paper for two minutes. Stretch, grab something to drink, or go outside and take a few deep breaths.

6. Come back to the sheet and notice if any of the values are similar or can be combined into an overarching idea. (For example, you might have diversity and inclusion listed as two separate values, but they can go under a broader heading of diversity, equity, and inclusion.)

7. Now cross out everything except for five of the values that are the most important to you.

Remember, just because you're crossing something out, that doesn't mean it's no longer important. You can have lots of values and things you hold near and dear to you. Identifying your core values just means that these values are going to become special collaborators in your business development journey. At least for now. Your values can change as you change, and as your business grows. But you need a starting point that you feel strongly about and that communicates the most important things your business believes in.

Once you know what your core values are, you need to spend some time developing a small statement or phrase to communicate to your teams, partners, customers, and clients what these ideas mean in the context of your company; words mean different things to different people. Again, my suggestion is to keep things short and sweet so that they can be useful tools that help you make decisions in your larger strategic decision making as well as in your day-to-day business operations.

USING YOUR ANTIRACIST LENS

Once you have determined your core values, you have to examine them through the lens of antiracism. Do the values that you've selected as part of your core values align with antiracist action or policy? Or have you selected values that increase the chances that you'll default into patterns of Whiteness? Remember, values like efficiency, independence, or competition might actually interrupt equity when you start to put those values into practice. They might cause you to skip steps in power sharing and collaboration or create feelings of isolation or conflict. This doesn't mean that you shouldn't choose these as core values; it just means that if these are truly your values, you'll need to implement explicit checks and balances to make sure that these values don't inadvertently violate your commitment to equity, inclusion, and antiracism.

USING YOUR VALUES AS A GUIDE

Once you have your core values selected, you'll want to make a practice of referring to them on a regular basis so that they become a go-to tool when you have to make decisions in your business, especially the hard ones. Again, these words aren't to become meaningless slogans—they should be operational and imperative in all your work. Your values can guide you in deciding how to spend your resources, including time, money, and human resources. What products or services to sell, or when to add more. Who to collaborate with, how to develop your marketing and outreach plans, how your company will handle sales processes, and especially how you'll handle difficult decisions like letting someone go, ending a product or service line, closing a location, or going fully remote or not.

> Not all values will be relevant to every decision you
> need to make, but if you select five core values, you
> will have at least one value that is supportive in just
> about every decision that you make.

Whenever clients ask me a question about what I think they should do, or how I think they should approach a problem, I first remind them of their values so that our conversation stays anchored in what they believe.

For example, I had a client share that one of their facilitators made a statement that was culturally insensitive, making a reference to entrepreneurs often feeling like a "slave to their work." Although this is a common, yet unfortunate, expression, this company had been engaged in DEI and antiracism work for over a year, and the facilitator knew right away that she didn't feel good about what she said on the call. Even though no one in the group made a complaint, the company knew that acting like the statement was never said would be unaligned with their commitment to creating a safe and inclusive environment for all of their current and future clients. After checking in, the company and facilitator decided that the action step that was most in alignment with their values and commitments would be to contact all the students, take responsibility for the statement that was made, explain why it was inappropriate and out of the realm of integrity, apologize, and offer the opportunity for any student to reach out if they had concerns or questions so that the facilitator could make amends personally.

APPLYING YOUR VALUES

To practice using your values in a decision-making process, you can write down some of the decisions you have to make, or the experiences you've had in your career and ask yourself, "How would I respond if I centered _____ value in this dilemma?" or "How could the value of _____ guide me in behaving in this scenario?"

Here are some common situations you might face in business that can get you started with practicing:

- How do I sell my products/services using a value of _____ (insert one of your values)?
- How do I approach a client who has defaulted on a payment using a value of _____?
- How do I reflect my value of _____ in our hiring process?
- If _____ is my core value, how do I approach a decision related to major shifts in my business?
- An employee is not performing their duties adequately. If my guiding value is _____, how do I approach this situation?

Being in a practice of asking how your values are showing up in all of the things you do, and all of the choices you make, will help you and your team maintain integrity. As you grow, you'll likely hire team members who report to you, and then eventually new team members will join who report to your leadership team. With every additional level of leadership in your business, there is a greater chance that people will become disconnected from your direct influence and intentions. This kind of values drift happens when you're just relying on people to stay in alignment with your company values the way that you do as the CEO, founder, or leader because they are good people and you trust them, instead of explicitly teaching your teams how to use the values and commitments as an internal reference point for their jobs and creating the intentional policies and practices to hold them accountable.

I suggest using the values application exercise frequently with your team as a meeting opener or icebreaker activity, and also by making the question "How would we respond if we center _____ (value)?" a go-to question during planning or problem solving whenever it seems relevant. This will make your values an active tool in your community and help your team members have a practical understanding of how your core values show up in your company on a day-to-day basis.

NOTE TO THE SOLOPRENEUR

I can hear some of you saying now, "But, Trudi, I'm a one-person operation. I don't even know if I want a team. How does this apply to me?" The good news is that whether you are a solopreneur trying to make consistent revenue so you can leave your main job or whether you are working at a multimillion-dollar corporation with a large team and layers of leadership, I can tell you this. . . . Everyone starts with their values.

In some ways, the work of getting clear on your core values and practicing using them in your decision-making process is even more significant as a solopreneur. When you're a one-person show, it's really easy for you to overwork, overpromise, make compromises for clients, become loose with setting boundaries because you're in hustle mode, and trying to balance building something you're passionate about with a real need to make money and pay the bills. I 100 percent understand that tension. So, when you're running the whole show and you haven't been in a practice of checking in with your values, sometimes you don't even realize you're out of alignment, and possibly out of integrity, from what you actually believe in until you've hit a wall. Misalignment can look like a few things, including burnout, a feeling of dread before you start a client call or working on a product you're designing, ongoing procrastination, being embarrassed by projects or clients you've taken on, or implementing a strategy that you don't really understand or agree with but that you're doing anyway because you've been told it's the right, effective, or best thing to do.

And sure, you might not have a team right now. You might not even be able to imagine what it will take to make that first hire. The thought of having a team might even be terrifying to you. But businesses are collaborative ventures, and you will more than likely come to a point in time where you need help with something. It might be that you need to hire a contractor to build your website, or an administrative assistant to get some things off your plate. Starting with your values and commitments as a solopreneur will help you start as you mean to go on and will provide you with the ability to have clear thoughts about these things before you have to train or collaborate with someone else.

MAKING COMMITMENTS TO DIVERSITY, EQUITY, INCLUSION, AND ANTIRACISM

The year 2020 brought many new social dynamics into our awareness and one of them is a heightened attention on DEI and antiracism in our society. Since that time, many more companies have released statements about their commitment to diversity, equity, inclusion, and antiracism. If you were scrolling through any social media platform in 2020, you would have seen company after company displaying their commitment with black squares on social media, sharing their stance with the #BlackLivesMatter movement, and even turning over their platforms to BIPoC creators and activists as a way to amplify Brown and Black voices. Suggestions from activists and leaders encouraged businesses to make their positions on these issues public, make statements, dedicate a portion of revenue to support Black businesses, have hiring quotas for staff and contacts that are part of marginalized communities, hire DEI educators for trainings, and commit to do "the work." These are all great suggestions, but they are also insufficient. All of these suggestions focus on what people should do, but not what they need to undo.

> Antiracism requires a lot of undoing before we can start doing.

Making a commitment means that you are making a promise and taking on the responsibility of carrying out an action, not just stopping or disagreeing with a behavior or action that you don't agree with. Making a commitment to antiracism means that you are committing to conducting yourself, and your business, in ways that do not exploit people, that center people who have been marginalized, and that create the kind of impact that leads to equity for all people. This also means that you will evaluate the things you think you know (or have been taught) about how to run a successful business, how to make money, and how to lead, and then you will examine the ways that these things contribute to or replicate racism, oppression, or marginalization of other people.

> Traditional business practices often have sneaky tactics that disguise oppression, exploitation, and marginalization as business as usual, touting them as widely accepted and normal policies and practices.

This can include things like silencing employees or former employees, abusing your power and position, attempting to control people's responses or behaviors, interfering with people's ability to earn money, using their gifts, exploiting someone's intellectual capital, requiring "other duties as assigned" policies, and placing an overemphasis on formal education to evaluate competence versus experience.

Here are some examples of what this can look like.

INAPPROPRIATE NON-DISCLOSURES

Some employers ask employees or clients to sign non-disclosure agreements that go beyond protecting a company's intellectual property. Sometimes these agreements are used to silence people from sharing stories of negative experiences they've had with an employer, colleague, or other client. These stories can include traumatic issues, or actions that demonstrate that the company does not carry out the values for which they advocate. This type of silencing is an act of oppression because the company is using its power and money to control a person who does not have the power.

INAPPROPRIATE NON-COMPETE CLAUSES IN WORK AGREEMENTS

Similar to a non-disclosure agreement, non-compete clauses are often used unjustly. When a company asks an employee or contractor to sign a non-compete agreement, it typically states that the employee can't work for another company during the time they are employed with the contracted employer, or for a period of time after the employment ends, or that the employee can't be in business for themselves for a period of time after. The justification for this type of contract is that it prevents the employee from working for a competitor and sharing company information or poaching clients from the employer. However, this type of contract only protects the entity with the most power—the employer.

If an employee is fired or laid off, if people aren't being compensated for full-time, well-over-living-wage employment, or if the employee was actually a contractor who should be treated as an independent business owner in the first place, non-competes should immediately be released. Non-competes should never be used as part of severance packages unless the company is paying a salary to the employee for the duration of their non-compete agreement. This is abuse of power, economic oppression, and is more than likely going to impact Black and Brown employees more severely than White employees.

VALUING FORMAL EDUCATION TO EVALUATE COMPETENCE VERSUS EXPERIENCE AND PERFORMANCE

If you want to be a brain surgeon, you'll have to go to medical school. If you want to practice law, you have to pass the bar. Some professions require a person to pass certain milestones in order to demonstrate mastery, and having that mastery can be a matter of life or death. But in most cases, requiring a degree, or using a degree as a metric of competence, is a way of keeping other people out. A college degree is not a guaranteed indicator that someone is a good fit for the job, has the right experience, or will be a good fit for your team.

This doesn't mean that pursuing higher education isn't important, or even that a college education isn't valuable. It only means that a college degree has value, and that life and work experience are also valuable. The ability to go to college is a privilege that not everyone has, and as college education costs rise, students are increasingly opting out and taking on the long-term, crushing debt that is associated with it. If we link employment to college degrees, college degrees will continue to widen the opportunity gap.

"OTHER DUTIES AS ASSIGNED"

The phrase "other duties as assigned" is basically a stand-in for your manager saying, "Your job is whatever I ask you to do." This creates opportunities for exploitation of people who have been hired to do certain things in which they have interest or expertise. For most people designing a job description, the phrase "other duties as assigned" brings to mind a variety of tasks that are at least tangentially related to a person's job, or the day-to-day operations of the business, such as committee meetings, supervising interns, and even taking turns throwing out the trash in small businesses that don't have a custodian in the office. However, in other cases, "other duties as assigned" turns into a variety of tasks that have nothing to do with a person's job, including picking up the boss's dry cleaning or cleaning the bathrooms. Doing your best to make a list in the job description of the tasks that a person might need to perform and being open to having conversations when something needs to be done that is not on the list creates a heightened level of transparency and openness, reducing the chances that someone in the company might take advantage of someone they supervise.

I'll add here, if you're the person reading this and thinking, "Well, people can't do that," "That doesn't happen," or "I would never do that to someone," you win the optimism award for this chapter. Let me assure you, these things—and worse—are happening every day.

Making a commitment to antiracism and equity means taking a look at some of these policies and practices that are rooted in oppressive ideas about people and their inherent value, and analyzing common practices that allow people with power to make decisions that impact the lives of others without regard for how those decisions impact the person with less power and privilege.

Our antiracist commitment requires us to replace these oppressive and exploitative practices with practices and policies that are more liberatory and just. Even when it's inconvenient. Even when some of

> the old ways might be good for your profit margins or
> allow you to control the narrative.

Being committed to antiracism means that everything is on the table for interrogation. It means being willing to look at all of the things you've learned, all of the things you've done and are currently doing, and opening yourself up to change.

PERFORMATIVE ACTION
VERSUS FULL ALIGNMENT

One of the biggest fears I hear from my clients about sharing their commitments and values is that they don't want to appear like they are being performative. "Performative allyship" is another one of the terms that we've heard more and more frequently over the last two years as entrepreneurs, businesses, and online brands have made public statements about their stances on issues of social and racial justice. Performative action means that the motivating factor in someone's action is external. They are engaged in a performance in order to show outsiders (audiences, potential clients, customers, partners, etc.) that they are committed to a cause or a belief because it's what the outsiders expect or want to see from them. This external motivation causes them to do things, like post to Instagram, swap out images on their website, or put together a panel on diversity, that looks and sounds good but are not authentic. The core purpose is to satisfy or placate an external group in order to increase one's social capital by appearing to be "with the shit."

Performative allyship often occurs when people are so eager to demonstrate their commitment to a cause that they skip the step of actually researching the issue fully or thinking through the ramifications of their actions. Take the hashtag "#BlackOutTuesday" for example. In June 2020, Jamila Thomas and Brianna Agyemang, two Black women working in the music industry, called for their colleagues to take a collective pause on Tuesday, June 2, and to take time to reflect on how they "as gatekeepers of culture" should hold each other accountable. They called for a day of disconnection from work and reconnection with their community. The hashtag "#BlackOutTuesday" was created for people participating in the #TheShowMustBePaused movement. What happened instead was, on June 2, celebrities and non-celebrities jumped on the bandwagon and started to share black squares on their feeds without fully understanding the intention or consequences. In addition, they posted #BlackLivesMatter, not realizing that this hashtag is used as a way to share information about political and social events impacting Black communities and the racial justice movement overall. The consequence of this misinformed action was that people who were sharing important information about the #BlackLivesMatter movement were not able to present their content to their followers because people had to scroll through endless black squares in order to access this information.

Performative allyship in the workplace can take many forms, including putting together a diversity committee to organize things like multicultural potluck dinners or putting on a "special assembly" during Black History month, but not providing employees with the authority or resources to actually create institutional change. It's organizing service trips abroad to build schools, or sharing pictures of your service work, but not supporting or even being aware of the ways that children are being inadequately educated in your local or nearby communities. It's putting a statement on your job description that says, "We encourage diverse candidates to apply," but shrugging your shoulders and saying, "We didn't get any qualified applicants of Color" when pressed about the lack of diversity on your team. It looks like hiring a DEI consultant to work with staff but leadership—including the CEO—is not in attendance.

So, how do you share your commitments to antiracism without being performative? Well, you do your work. Doing your work means creating the structural changes in your company that support your commitments and values. It means taking on the personal journey of unpacking your bias, privilege, and Whiteness. It looks like releasing the need for urgency and taking the time to understand and do things right.

| Remember: Urgency interrupts equity.

When you feel like you need to take an urgent action, like posting a black square on Instagram because you don't want your community to think you don't support Black Lives, you are definitely being performative. But even beyond that, you open yourself up to making mistakes that have bigger downsides than waiting. Instead, you should take the time to understand the issues and make sure that whatever you decide to do is in aligned action, even if what you do isn't public-facing.

The beauty about being in full alignment is that you release your need to care about what someone else thinks, because you've created a business (and life, for that matter) in which your commitments and values are clearly embedded in what you do and how you do it, so people don't have to wonder about where you stand. And when you do make a public statement, or take a stand for or against something, it is because you have considered the issue, you're well informed, and you've made thoughtful choices about how to move forward. When you get to this level of alignment, you don't care if someone thinks you're being performative, because you're not motivated by what people think. You're no longer engaged in a performance.

WHAT ARE YOUR COMMITMENTS?

You might have some burning commitments that you're just ready to post on your website and share with the world, but before you take rash action, sit with your commitments and ask yourself if you are truly aligned with them—not just in "thoughts and prayers," but in action. Sometimes we feel committed to something, but we aren't in a place to be able to consistently carry out that commitment. When that happens, I suggest writing up a list of commitments that you can make right now, and then another list for future commitments. For example, you might feel a strong desire to commit a portion of your revenue to a charity, but for new entrepreneurs, who might not yet be covering their basic needs, carrying out that commitment might cause an unreasonable amount of stress or burden on them or their new business. Instead of making the commitment to donate a portion of your revenue to charity, you might consider dedicating time to the same cause, or raising money outside your business to donate.

I also suggest being specific about what your commitments are so that you, and others, are clear about the actions that are expected as a result of that commitment. A company saying that they're committed to antiracism or diversity, equity, and inclusion is very different from a company saying, "We are committed to ensuring that a minimum 20 percent of our spending goes into Black and Brown communities through our hiring, giving, and contracting." One of these statements is a general statement that reflects their ideological commitments, and the other is a statement that is specific and measurable.

If you're ready, grab another sheet of paper or open up a document and write down a few things that you feel committed to. Once you're done with your list, sit with each statement and ask yourself the following questions:

- **Is this commitment ideological or actionable?** If its ideological, figure out a way to modify the commitment to make it more action oriented.

- **Is this commitment measurable? How will I, or others, know that we are executing this commitment in our business operations?** If you find that your commitment is not measurable, think about how you can modify the statement so that you or members of your team can measure your progress against it.

- **Is this a commitment that I am ready to make right now, or is this commitment more aspirational?** If the commitment is aspirational, modify your commitment so that it can reflect your first steps. You might also consider a statement that indicates where you'll take your commitment in the future. For example:

  We are committed to providing living wages, and full health benefits to our team members. As our revenue grows, we will incrementally increase our salaries proportionate to our revenue, dedicating 30 percent of our total revenue to our staff costs. We will operate with the leanest team possible in order to pay our team equitably, while working to create balanced workloads.

  This commitment demonstrates a company's commitment to growth and improvement over time, while demonstrating a thoughtfulness about the balance between salary, leanness, and workload.

- **Who should I share these with first? Who else has ownership over these commitments?** Before posting your commitments online, ask yourself if there are other people on your team or in your community who might have some responsibility in taking action on these commitments. Bring this work to those people, share your ideas, and engage in a conversation about what it means to have these commitments and what it will take to carry them out. Be open to modifying or adding things based on this feedback, but only if the changes bring you closer to your values. You shouldn't feel pressured to change commitments that compromise or dilute your values.

■ **When should I (or we) publicly share these?** Take your time to think this through. Remember, this isn't about who's running the fastest race in the "woke Olympics." This is about thoughtfulness, intention, and alignment. This also doesn't mean that you should do nothing or wait endlessly. It just means that you should give yourself enough time to evaluate what needs to be in place before you share your commitments. For example, if you have a large workforce, you should share this with your employees before posting it on Instagram, or if you say you're making structural changes to a system that actually requires support from a board of directors, you first need to enroll them in your vision.

CREATING YOUR VALUES AND COMMITMENTS COLLABORATIVELY

If you happen to be building a business with a team, or if you're building the kind of business that has a board of directors, all of this work should be done collaboratively. Collaborative work takes longer, but it's a worthy and often transformational experience under the right facilitation. If you don't have a facilitator, my suggestion is to bring these exercises to the group and have everyone work on them individually. Then, break into groups of two, share your work with each other, and develop a collaborative set of values and commitments that represents ideas from both partners. From there, partner up again with another group of two and go through the process again. Take the ideas of both partner sets and then combine them into one collective set of values and commitments. You can continue this process until the whole group has shared with each other and you have one set of values and one set of commitments that represent the contributions and dialogue of all the members of the team.

Take this last set of values and commitments, write them on some chart paper on a wall, or on a blank document if you're working digitally, and make sure that everyone's voice is represented, that people can live with any compromises that have been made, that there are no critical omissions, and, of course, that your commitments and values meet antiracist standards.

For a long time, businesses (and nonprofits) have claimed that they uphold certain standards and values, emblazoning them on websites, merchandise, and in annual reports. They made promises to loyalty and progress, to vision and integrity, but ultimately their practices only deepened income inequality, unfair labor practices, and the continued systemic inequities based on income, race, and gender. For the new antiracist business leader, commitments and values are true guides, providing companies with quantifiable practices in antiracism and raising the bar not just for their leaders and staff, but for all companies doing business in their industry.

This isn't about performative business practices. This isn't about "out-woking" the competition. It is about becoming liberatory leaders who are able to establish commitments and values that create a new "business as usual," one in which decisions aren't made in silos or are disconnected from the consequences of oppression, but rather reflect intentional presence, thoughtfulness, and alignment with antiracist practices.

To that end, businesses are able to create an antiracist business model, redefining how they do business and creating a template for others to follow.

CHAPTER 6

ANTIRACIST BUSINESS MODELS

reating a model really just means that you're creating a theoretical framework for how you believe your business will operate. It's an example, just as you would draw out a rendering of a house before it's built or create a small-scale "model" of a mural before you paint it on the side of a building. Once upon a time, and in some cases still today, you'll need to represent that model in a formal business plan that would lay out all the details of your business including the products and services, market research, financial projections, and even your staffing plan. When people are starting businesses that require formal fundraising, or taking out traditional loans, these kinds of plans are still used. But today, most small businesses and entrepreneurs that are starting small really just need something simple to capture their ideas and share them easily with collaborators.

In a traditional business model, the approach is typically to see how a company can maximize profits and minimize costs, while keeping a level of quality and service with which the entrepreneur is satisfied. If you're reading this book, I would make a bet that you've had enough life experience to know that different companies have different standards for what kind of "quality" they can live with. Some companies sacrifice profit margins in order to deliver a higher level of customer service while others have the opposite reputation. In an antiracist business model, the bar is higher. The goal is to develop a plan for your overall business operations and revenue projections in addition to setting other goals that address your diversity, equity, inclusion, and social impact goals.

In antiracist business planning, you also get to revisit your business structure as a legal entity, how you earn and spend money, your financial projections, and what other measures of success you want to be accountable to in addition to the financial success. If you'd like a PDF download of a tool that you can use to brainstorm your antiracist business model, you can access the antiracist business model canvas along with other resources for this book at: www.antiracistbusinessbook.com.

If you are not new in business and are already familiar with these concepts, and currently have a business plan or model that you're following, I recommend thinking about how your business planning process was similar or dissimilar and consider how you would have done things differently if you were approaching the process with an antiracist lens. There is always the opportunity to revisit and grow in a new direction, so even if some of this seems familiar I encourage you to trust the process.

THE DIFFERENCE BETWEEN A BUSINESS MODEL AND A BUSINESS PLAN

A business plan is a document that an entrepreneur or team of entrepreneurs develops that lays out a complete description of the company that they are building. A plan typically includes between five and seven sections and can be used by the founders to pitch potential investors or apply to funding opportunities. Business plans are also used by the team to keep them focused on their intentions and to serve as a guide for how the business should be run in order to hit certain milestones. Sections of a business plan include a business description, staff/leadership structure, market research, competitive analysis, detailed descriptions of products and services, marketing plans, sales structures, a full financial projection of your revenue, costs, and profits over five years, and an executive summary, which is a high-level overview of the entire document.

If you're building a business that is going to require you to pitch investors or apply for a loan, you will need to write a business plan. There are many websites and books that can walk you through the ins and outs of a standard business plan, but for most entrepreneurs who are looking to start a small business, you can probably wait on this step, if not skip it altogether.

What can't be skipped is developing a sound business model. Generally, business models are like a shorthand for understanding how a company operates. The model is like a one- or two-page business outline that helps you get clear on a few critical components of your business idea: 1) what you'll sell, 2) how you'll sell it, 3) what it will cost for your business to operate, and 4) how you will make money. The model you choose for your business will dictate how you approach all other aspects of your work. Here are some examples of business models that you are likely familiar with as consumers:

■ **The franchise model.** With the franchise business model, you are buying into a business that is already established. This means you can't stray from the business practices that were put in place by the franchisor. This model is a commercial and legal agreement between the owner (the franchisor) and the individual (the franchisee).[1] Some examples include McDonald's, Dunkin', and Anytime Fitness.

▪ **The freemium model.** This is an increasingly popular model, which offers some free service or access to limited features on a digital product—like an app or a game— then charges for upgraded, premium services, or to increase the ease of use by charging to eliminate ads.

▪ **The subscription model.** Subscription-based business models provide a product or service in return for an annual or monthly subscription fee. The focus of this model is customer retention over acquisition. Examples of this business model are magazine and newspaper subscriptions, vitamin subscriptions in which the vitamins are automatically mailed to your home, health and wellness apps or programs, and audiobooks.

▪ **The direct-sales model.** In the direct-sales business model, you are selling products directly to the client. As opposed to retail marketing, in which companies buy large quantities of products to display in their stores and allow the customer to shop and choose for themselves, direct sales is more of a boots-on-the-ground operation. While the direct-sales model isn't inherently bad, some predatory companies use this model to exploit aspiring entrepreneurs. These companies, also known as MLMs, get paid when their independent salespeople buy products and recruit other salespeople to buy products. Whether or not their products sell to customers who actually benefit from them is inconsequential. Salespeople are promised commission when they recruit more salespeople to buy products with the hope of selling them later.

- **Platform model.** Another model that could be fine if we applied antiracist principles but has been disproportionately exploitative and predatory is the platform model, used by companies such as Uber and Lyft. In this model, the company creates and promotes the platform service, but the service is being delivered by people who are not employees of the company.
- **Retail model.** Retailers are the companies that sell products to consumers through their store operations. Retailers are usually selling products that they did not make themselves; rather, they curate items that fit within the store's brand and business concept. Sometimes retailers are selling products that another part of their company has manufactured. Victoria's Secret is an example of this. Their retail stores only sell their own product lines, and you can't buy their products in other stores.
- **Manufacturing model.** Manufacturing companies are the makers of just about everything we have. Manufacturing is the process of turning raw materials into finished goods. There are all types of manufacturers across industries, including tech, food, wood, metal, cars, chemicals, and medicine. You name it, someone is making it. Manufacturing is typically working in conjunction with retailers who sell their manufactured products, but some manufacturers have an internal retailing arm to sell directly to consumers.
- **Service-based model.** In this model, the clients are purchasing a service that you provide rather than a product. Within this sector, you can operate using the done-for-you model (company provides the service for the customer), done-with-you model (company assists the customer in completing a project or goal), or the training

model (where the company trains or supports the customer to accomplish their need on their own).

It's important to note that ultimately it's the people behind the companies that uphold systems, and who create and carry out policies that are rooted in oppression, exploitation, bias, prejudice, and so on. So, when we talk about an antiracism practice, we need to be thinking about both the models we are choosing and the ways that people in these businesses are carrying out their actions. Although some of these business models lend themselves to being more flexible to implementing antiracist policies and practices, others tend to be more inherently exploitative and oppressive.

In network marketing, individuals become representatives of a product that they sell directly to consumers through their personal and/or professional networks. The rep is given marketing materials and strategy support by the company, but the representatives are responsible for generating their own leads in order to sell products. The success of network marketing is dependent on the representative being able to recruit other representatives under them, which is often called building a "downline." The rep recruits other representatives, who then recruit other representatives, and each rep earns a percentage of sales that each person in their downline sells, and also gets paid bonuses for any other representatives that are recruited in their line. What often happens is that the sole priority of a representative is to recruit other reps instead of selling the product themselves, and in many cases there is little demand for the product the company sells, outside of the reps themselves who will use the products as their own case study.

Network marketing is an example of a model that has an inherent inequity built into the system. First off, network marketing is often promoted to people as a business opportunity where people will be an entrepreneur or start their own business, but the fact is that most reps are salespeople for a company of which they do not have ownership. This lack of transparency and often blatant misrepresentation can create hardship for people whose personal networks are less resourced, especially when the costs for participating in these companies can be steep.

In 2016, Herbalife came to a $200 million settlement after an investigation found that the company misled their representatives with claims that representatives could quit their jobs and earn more money and make "big bucks." Reps were encouraged to become leaders in the company by investing their own money into brick-and-mortar storefronts called "Nutrition Clubs" where people would not just come to purchase Herbalife products but were also pitched to become part of the reps' downline. What the lawsuit alleged is that Herbalife products were being primarily sold to other representatives, meaning that there was little to no demand for the products outside of the representative networks themselves, which is a violation of federal law.[2]

Are all network marketing companies the same? No. Because nothing ever works like that. Many people involved in network marketing businesses have a wide variety of experiences with their companies, but if network marketing is a business model you are exploring, you should know that this is one of those models that has built-in inequities that you'll probably have little influence over as a representative, because you are not the business owner. If your plan is to develop a new product or service that will be sold using a network marketing model, I think there is a huge opportunity to consider how it can be designed to increase transparency, employ more equitable practices, and develop antiracist policies.

As a contrast to network marketing, let's look at the freemium model where the structure of the model itself is less inherently oppressive. Freemium models are most often encountered in the software/tech/app space where the company provides a valuable service or product for free to its users but limits the number of features the user has access to or limits the capacity of the product. Once the user reaches the limits of the product's capacity or decides that they want access to the advanced features, they can upgrade to a paid version of the product or service.

ConvertKit is a software company providing a range of services to creators and small business owners including email marketing technology, landing pages, and e-commerce tools to companies of all sizes. Their basic package is totally free for users who have an email list of under one thousand subscribers and includes email broadcasts, landing pages on which people can use to build sales pages or basic websites, and the ability to sell products and digital subscriptions. As users grow their list past one thousand subscribers, the price of their subscription goes up, and if users want to add more premium features, including advanced automations, funnels, and the ability to integrate their software with others, then they can move into a number of paid packages.

But for a creator who is starting out at the beginning, having access to free tools can be exactly what they need to build the momentum to start moving their business forward. ConvertKit also has an affiliate program for people who love their product. This allows ConvertKit community members to share the platform with others and earn a recurring commission on user subscriptions each month. Unlike network marketing, there isn't an obligation to share the platform and user success doesn't rely on the user's ability to get other people to sign up. The affiliate program is something a user can opt into if they desire.

In addition to being a great example of what's possible with a freemium model, ConvertKit is also very values aligned, and has a stated commitment to diversity, equity, and inclusion. You can check out my podcast interview on *Business Remixed* with ConvertKit's chief operations officer to learn more.

Hopefully, by now you have a good idea of what business models are and are starting to identify what business model you have or are trying to build. But a business model is not a business—it's just an idea, and there are many more components of your business that we need to look at to ensure that you're building a business model that is centered around equity, making an intentional impact, and practicing antiracism.

WHO DO YOU SERVE?

The next step is to think about your ideal clients and customers, but before we start I want to openly and honestly discuss something that I wish someone would have told me much earlier in my entrepreneurial journey: your customer, your client, and the person you most want to help might be different people.

There's a good chance that if you're reading this book, you're one of those people who really wants to change the world. You see a problem that you want to fix, or maybe you've experienced a hardship and now you want to relieve the hardships of others like you. This may be the driving force in your business. And you may feel stalled because you think that the people you want to help most don't have the money to pay you to help them fix the problem. And you might be right. But you're looking at it all wrong, and understanding the difference between your customer, your client, and the people you most want to help might be the thing that gets you unstuck.

> The community of people that you want to help the most is what I call an "impact community." This is a community that you feel a deep connection to and to which you want to contribute so significantly that the conditions of their lives become better by your contribution.

An impact community is different from a social justice cause that you're involved in because causes can sometimes be more general and issue-based, such as prison reform or autism awareness, whereas your impact community is specific and person-centered, like the children attending the under-resourced school in a community you care about, or Black and Brown underemployed millennials.

For many of us, we set out to start a business because we want to help our impact community. And we can absolutely, 100 percent do this. But our impact community may not be, and does not need to be, our customer or our client. Confusing this point is the very thing that stalled my progress by a few years because I was following the advice from coaches and thought leaders that told me to find something I was passionate about and start a company doing that. The problem was, my primary passion at that time was adolescent development and helping youth from inner cities, like the one I grew up in, overcome the barriers that were keeping them stuck. Following my mentors' advice, I set out and designed amazing programs for teens, becoming certified as a youth life coach to supplement all my years of studying positive youth development, and working in youth development programming in nonprofits. The problem was that inner-city youth do not have money to hire a coach, and the nonprofits I was pitching did not have enough money to pay me for my programs in a way that would be effective, let alone profitable.

Once I realized that my business model was not going to facilitate the kind of impact I wanted to make, I was able to see that my customer, my client, and my impact community were three different segments.

Clients or end-users in product-based businesses are the people who ultimately use the product or services, often solving a problem that your clients or end-users have. For example, if I go get my nails done at a nail salon, I am the client at the salon. When my team and I go into a yearlong coaching process with the leadership team of a company, the members of that leadership team are our clients.

The customer, who might be a client, is the person who has the authority to hire and pay you. I know that this might be a different definition to the word "customer" than you might think, but many people I've worked with have found this slight reframe incredibly helpful. If we think about our customer as the person who has authority to hire us, our client as the person who is using our product or service, and our impact community as the people we want to help the most, we can start to see business models, and revenue streams, that we could not see when we were still under the impression that our impact community had to be our customer.

Consider this: If you provide a service to children and you think that children are your customer, it's going to drive you to create marketing content and solutions to problems that appeal to children. But children tend not to have money of their own to spend. If we think of adult caretakers (parents, extended families, teachers, etc.) as our customers, and their children as our clients, it helps us approach the rest of our work with a clear sense of who we have to talk to when we're selling, and how to design our product or service for the child who is ultimately the user.

Let's take it one step further. Let's say you're a teacher and you want to start a business that provides tutoring services to low-income students. If you try and approach this thinking that the school itself or the families who are low-income are your ideal customers, you're going to have an uphill battle making any progress or money. But if we think of them as the impact community, then we can start to develop services and products that can be sold to customers that have related needs, and who also might be excited about working with a company that has this mission of increasing access to tutoring. You could sell tutoring services to families that have flexible income and regularly pay for tutoring and other enrichment activities for their children. You can potentially run that tutoring in groups in order to maximize your earnings per hour and then distribute some of the revenue by paying tutors in the under-resourced school.

In 2016, while I was transitioning out of working my full-time nonprofit job, I knew that the population of people I wanted to help would not be able to pay enough for coaching and consulting fees to replace the income I would lose once I left my job. However, I could not be okay with leaving my job to make hundreds of dollars an hour and leave my friends, colleagues, and community members behind without sharing some of the lessons that I had learned over the years. I was committed to helping Black and Brown millennial women build businesses to supplement their incomes by learning the skills, and also building the confidence and mindset, necessary to take more ownership of their life and earning power. I set up a business model that allowed me to offer consulting and coaching to schools, nonprofits, and social entrepreneurs who were able to make a significant investment in my services, and then I designed the BeABoss program that would serve my impact community.

The first year I ran BeABoss, I charged between twenty and fifty dollars a month per person. The money generated through the program paid for a full breakfast for every session, covered the rent of the meeting space we used for our meetings, and paid a stipend for a program assistant who helped facilitate content and do some administrative tasks. In 2020, when the program went virtual due to COVID-19, and my company saw a spike in revenue due to the interest in antiracist education, we immediately canceled all the participants' payment plans and ran the program virtually and for free for the remainder of the year because we knew that the economic impacts of the pandemic where likely going to be more severe for our clients in that program.

BeABoss never had the burden of generating a profit because it was always intended to be an impact initiative that the company would support. Some of the people who went through that program did incredible things, including starting a multidisciplinary arts production company, consulting and training businesses, and forming private therapy practices. We also had significant job advancements, people returned to grad school, people left bad relationships, and others got the courage to take their first solo vacations. Of course, the program can't take total credit for all of these things, but I've had plenty of participants reach out to me over the years to share how the program impacted their trajectory.

The folks in BeABoss were not my customers, and they were more than clients. They were, and are, a community of people that I deeply cared about, many of whom I have become friends with. They were my community.

I hope for many of you that this shift in the way you think about a customer, a client, and an impact community helps to widen your scope of the different types of people you can serve. Now that we've straightened that out, let's talk about your ideal customers.

IDEAL CUSTOMERS

In a lot of business programs, you'll be encouraged to develop a customer avatar, or ideal customer profile. In these exercises, entrepreneurs are encouraged to develop a detailed character that represents their target customer, including a narrative about this fictional character's life down to their name, age, whether they have children, whether they're married, how they spend their days, how much money they make, and so on. What has always been interesting to me is that most of these activities don't prompt entrepreneurs to explicitly name a person's race, which, based on my experience working with entrepreneurs over the last five years, is because a lot of people who facilitate these types of activities take a color-blind approach to the work.

> Here's the thing: When we're using this approach of a customer avatar, in any places where we don't fill in explicit details about the person we're creating, our mind is going to fill those gaps in for us. When our minds have to do this work, the gaps are filled with default information. Can you guess what default information our minds use? Ourselves.

So, unless you are intentionally creating something, or selling to someone that is *not* you, you're probably using yourself as your ideal customer avatar.

On a recent trip to facilitate an equity team training for a client, this very phenomenon revealed itself. During the training, we were talking about our clients' customer avatars. One of the newer members to the team said that their interpretation of the avatar was "White women with money." Immediately the CEO said, "No one ever said White." The team then discussed how, although no one ever said their avatar should be a White woman, the general image that came to everyone's mind was in fact White. We then went on to imagine how things could be different if it were clear that the ideal customers were a diverse set of women who had shared values, problems, and dreams, instead of shared identity demographics.

The purpose of this exercise is to help marketers understand who they are selling their product or service to, and good marketers know that developing marketing strategies and materials involves speaking to one specific person. This "speaking to one person" approach is meant to make the tasks related to marketing less overwhelming, because if you sit down to create a sales email for one person who you know intimately, it feels easier than crafting an email to be sent to a lot of people. But we can have the same effect by thinking about our customers as members of a community who share values, dreams, frustrations, desires, barriers, and challenges, instead of creating an avatar around a demographic type. The demographic approach ultimately can lead you down a path of creating an audience of homogenous customers and clients and can increase the chances that you are using stereotypes and biases to inform your ideas of who you think people are.

Here are some questions that are meant to help you build your community avatar and lead you to a more diverse, representative community of clients, audience members, and customers:

- What qualities or life experiences do your ideal clients have?
- How might your clients' lives be different from each other?
- What values do your ideal clients share with each other that are also shared with the company?
- What inspires them?
- What angers or frustrates them?
- What do your clients stand behind?
- Who do you hope shows up?
- Who do you hope opts out?

Once you think through these questions, you can develop your customer communities and avatars, and you can even give them individual names and personalities. I suggest making a few of them to represent ways they might be different and being extra clear on their shared characteristics.

Getting clear on who you serve is just as important as getting clear on what you sell, whether that's a service, a product, a work of art, or a food item. This narrowing down of your audience is the very thing that will help you become successful. It's a misconception that the way to make more money is to come up with a business idea that is going to serve everyone. The most successful businesses are the ones that get clear on who their customers are and then create products and experiences that are specific to their customers' tastes, values, and preferences.

LEGAL STRUCTURES

I can't tell you how many conversations I've had with people who want to start a business but they get delayed by things that really shouldn't prevent them from getting started. A few of those things are business cards, websites, and legal documents. I'll just say this to get it out of the way: you *do not* need a business card or a website to start a business. But I will take some time to demystify business structures for you, because it takes time to consider them. Many people think they can't start their business until they have filed some paperwork, and that is rarely the case. But filing and registering your business as a legal entity is a good idea in order to separate your business liabilities from becoming your own personal liabilities. What I want to point out about legal structures is that, like business models, no single structure is inherently less racist, because it's the people and the policies that determine whether or not the business is modeling antiracist values.

Here are the common types of legal structures that you probably do business with every day. To determine the best type of legal structure for your business, you should consult with a CPA or business attorney who can talk to you about your specific situation since tax implications will be different based on the structure you choose.

- Sole proprietorship: A business in which an individual owns an unincorporated business.[3]
- Limited Liability Company (LLC): A company that protects the business owners from personal responsibility for debts or liabilities.
- S-corporation: A business that passes its income, losses, credits, and tax deductions to its shareholders so they can include them on their individual tax forms. This helps them avoid paying taxes twice—once at the corporate level, and once again individually.[4]
- B-corporation: An up-and-coming kind of business that values purpose, as well as profit. B-corps are legally required to take into account the impact of their business practices with regard to labor, consumers, community, and the environment.[5]
- Nonprofit organizations: These companies advance social causes and provide a public benefit and are not required to pay taxes as they deliver goods and services without payment.[6]
- Worker-owned co-ops: A business in which the workers own, operate, and vote on the board of directors.[7]
- Corporations: A legal entity that is considered separate from its owners, also known as a "legal person."[8] Shareholders may enjoy profits but are not personally liable for the company's debts.

None of these legal structures are inherently racist or equitable, good or evil. It's the way in which these systems are weaponized by capitalism that poisons the well. For instance, sole proprietorships place the power with the individual business owner. However, Black and other marginalized people are routinely denied business loans, therefore preventing them from starting or maintaining their businesses.[9] Although minoritized people make up 32 percent of the population, they account for only 18 percent of business owners.[10] We've already discussed the lack of Black and Brown leadership in nonprofits. Even something as seemingly equitable as worker co-ops have to work at antiracism because they are born out of a systemically racist society.[11] Until our society is liberated from the chains of White supremacy, there is no business model or legal structure that is impervious to racism. Therefore, every business model needs to have diversity from top to bottom, in addition to fully integrated antiracist values.

Again, it's not the model that makes a business either racist or antiracist. I intentionally titled this chapter "Antiracist Business Models" because I get so many questions about the best business models for impact-driven entrepreneurs. People ask, "Should I just start a nonprofit?" or "Is a B-corp the best way to ensure that my company stays on track?" or "I'm interested in a co-op, but I don't have people who are interested in starting one with me. Should I just wait?" In the end, it's always the people, policies, and procedures that determine how a business is run. Antiracist business models build in structural safeguards to increase the likelihood of our ultimate goal: equity. Equity at the workplace for team members, equitable access for customers and clients, and deep and committed values alignment. If you can start by creating an intentional values-driven culture, and policies and procedures that help guide your business toward an antiracist future, you will be part of a new business economy that contributes to global racial justice efforts.

But first, you must build the space to make that possible.

CHAPTER 7

CREATE INTENTIONAL SPACE

In 2011, I was still trying to convince myself that the best thing I could do with my career was change the system from the inside. So, I did what most youth development professionals do. I applied for a job in my local school district. It was the same district in which I had dropped out fifteen years earlier. I saw a job posting for what they called a Graduation Specialist, which was basically a case manager/support person for students who were "over age and under credit." I felt very well equipped for this job. First of all, I had been one of these students. I came from a similar background, I had barriers to high school completion that I'd managed to navigate, and on top of all that, I was finishing up my master's degree writing about effective youth programming for "high-risk" youth. It felt like this job was supposed to be mine.

I applied and was called in for a series of interviews that took place at the board of education's office, meeting with a variety of school principals who all told me what a dynamic program this was going to be, giving the students the support they needed to be successful. There would be community partnerships, bus passes, enrichment programs, small cohorts, credit recovery programs, and of course (highly trained) graduation specialists who would work with a small group of students. I was super excited, and although I was not thrilled by the idea of needing to be at work at 7:30 a.m., I decided it was worth it.

My first day of school was a few weeks into the new school year. I arrived eager to meet the students and the people I'd be working with, folks who I presumed would have the same passion for working with students as I did. I showed up to the office and the overwhelmed secretary asked one of the students in the office to walk me to the "Student Success Center."

We walked down stairwells and through hallways all the way to the opposite end of the building. And then we walked into the basement—you know, where all success stories come from. The student pointed to a door, where a garbage can sat, catching water from the leaking ceiling. I walked through the door and saw a space that reminded me of the welfare offices I used to have to sit in years before. There was a wall of windows that you couldn't open or see out of, a series of small rooms that were not large enough to be formal classrooms, and then a large room in the middle with tables, chairs, and computers. And it was cold. Really cold. The students were all wearing various hoodies and sweaters to keep warm, even if that meant they would get into trouble for not wearing their uniform.

I wanted to leave as soon as I got there. And as I would learn over the coming weeks, the students felt the same way. They were not fully integrated into the student body; instead, they were othered in a myriad of ways, from not being able to easily take classes with the general student population, to being physically separated from them, and, ultimately, to being exiled to the poorest physical environment on campus, despite there being plenty of space in the rest of the building.

Now, obviously I was not a part of the planning for the program, or part of the decision making when someone decided, "Hey . . . I know, let's put the kids with the most challenges and barriers to success in the worst space in the school so that they can be isolated from the rest of the students. That should help them feel supported and increase their chances of success." Although I don't think that was literally said, I do think that there was some unarticulated bias about who these students were and that this bias subconsciously impacted many decisions. Either way, it was clear that there wasn't much thought put into the physical, psychological, or emotional environment that was needed in order to increase the chances that all of the resources that were being put into the program would be effective.

I didn't last long. There were a lot of other policy and procedure issues that were in direct conflict with my values—and also with good practices for youth development—so I resigned after six months. But I was able to stay long enough to advocate for the students to be moved to a more appropriate part of the building, which took place over the winter holiday break. Though some changes do happen from the inside, antipathy and implicit bias far too often make the decisions. The spaces we create can communicate all kinds of subtle or explicit messages that will have different impacts on different people. When we talk about institutional racism, we're speaking about the ways that discrimination is codified not just in our rules and regulations but also in our internal decisions and designs. Far too often, the promise of good programming and progressive strategies gets felled not by lack of budget (as I've seen, the nonprofit industrial complex can certainly raise the funds), but by a lack of attention and care and, more often than not, the deep institutional biases that frequent decision making.

As antiracist entrepreneurs and leaders, we need to be mindful about the spaces we are creating and inviting people into, whether that is a new business, a program, project, or even just a workshop that will take a few hours to facilitate.

There are many messages that we communicate through some of the simplest choices we make that can either uphold toxic power dynamics and unhealthy cultures or establish healthy, participatory communities that make people feel welcomed and included.

We create space though our rules and agreements, our language, the way we welcome and onboard people (or don't) into a space or community, how we facilitate that space, how we manage power dynamics, the guidance that we provide to people about how to show up and be successful in a space, and what we do if and when things are disrupted or need to change.

Facebook and other tech giants are known for their ability to create physical spaces that foster very intentional workplace cultures. Facebook offices have open-concept workspaces that foster collaboration and community and also provide private spaces so team members can have quiet places for focused work. Art, natural light, and intentional interior design are incorporated throughout the offices, gyms, and outdoor spaces, including a rooftop garden at the company's headquarters, and free, high-quality food is supplied. Not only do the spaces create intentional culture, but they also eliminate the need for people to leave the office. The spaces that these tech giants create are successful reflections of precisely what the companies want to foster including productivity, innovation, and collaboration. It's worth pointing out, however, that just because the physical spaces are beautiful and effective and creating an intentional environment, they are not antiracist spaces that foster diversity, equity, and inclusion.

Dress codes are another way to create space because clothes can be a marker of status, professionalism, and culture. What we wear, and what we require others to wear, impacts the way people behave, feel, and think about one another. Because of this, you might decide that there are times when you need to provide dress codes, or dress guidelines, in order to create a particular vibe. When my team and I facilitate in-person trainings with corporate institutions, we send them a message telling them to dress casually and suggest that they not wear formal business attire like suits, ties, or high heels even if that is how they regularly show up for work. The programming that we facilitate with clients is already uncomfortable enough and pushes people to reconsider how standard practices and formalities like dress codes might be upholding Whiteness and reinforcing power imbalances. It's harder for people to have those conversations when their closest physical environment, the clothes they are wearing, is in direct conflict with the space we are trying to create. Asking people to wear nontraditional clothes to work sets the stage for having them participate in a nontraditional business workshop.

One of my favorite examples of non-verbal cues like dress and design to communicate the values of a space are restaurants. Imagine you are walking down a street lined with restaurants and you're trying to decide where you and your friend would like to eat dinner. You approach a restaurant, and you can see that the restaurant has white tablecloths, wineglasses on the set tabletops, and waitstaff with pressed white button-down shirts. These images are enough information for you to form an impression of the type of restaurant this is and what kind of experience you might have. Now, imagine you walk up to the menu mounted in one of the windows and you notice that the menu does not list any prices. A menu with no prices, along with the white tablecloths and formal waitstaff attire, sends a very explicit message. If you need to know the prices, this restaurant is not for you. If you decide to go into that restaurant, you are likely going to have an experience that is very aligned with the values related to fine dining. If you try to go into that restaurant in a tank top and flip-flops, you might be asked to leave.

Many people I speak to about this wonder: *Is that fair? Should there even be any dress codes at all? Is it equitable for a restaurant to ask someone to leave if they are wearing a tank top and flip-flops?* Well, I think the answer to that is yes. As I've pointed out, the clothes we wear contribute to the creation of intentional space. What would not be equitable is if the dress code required that guests wear a particular brand of clothes, instead of a type. For example, there have been times in my life where I've gone to a restaurant that was a stretch for my budget, but I was dressed within the dress code and my money was green too. If they required that I had on a Chanel suit in order to eat there, that would be inequitable.

Also, flip-flops are not a marginalized identity.

CREATING AN INTENTIONAL CULTURE

Space creation isn't just about giving people a set of community guidelines or sending a welcome packet in the mail. The core part of space creation is really a question of culture. What is the culture we are building in our space and for this community? This leads us to the question, "What is culture, anyway?" Culture is the word we use to describe a broad set of behaviors, beliefs, and ways of being that belong to a group or a subgroup of people. Cultures always emerge among a group or society. The ingredients to culture basically boil down to three core factors. The first is our social environment. This is the way that humans live together in groups and conduct our interpersonal relationships, and how we organize ourselves to get things done, whether that's to raise a family, build a house, run a business, or ensure that our species lives on. Within our social environments and relationships, we make rules for how we work together or against one another in order to achieve our collective goals.

In a business, the common goals of the social environment may include the sustainability of the business so that everyone stays employed, but it can also be about how a company delivers its products and services to people who really need them. The way people feel committed and connected to these shared goals along with the way the goals are carried out will have an influence on the culture of business. Other ways that our social environments impact business culture are the decisions we make about how formal and inclusive we are when we speak to each other. If I walked into a room and said, "Good morning, ladies and gentlemen. Thank you for coming here today," that would give off a very different impression than if I said, "Hey, y'all, thanks for having me today." The ways we relate to each other and work together are one way we produce culture.

Another factor that creates culture is our ecological environment, which can be thought of as both the physical and environmental spaces in which we exist, including all of the resources that are found there. Climate, for instance, is a perfect example of how our environments produce cultural traits. Communities of people who live in tropical climates have very distinct cultures from those in cold climates. For example, the climate has a direct impact on the foods that become incorporated as traditional "cultural foods." Food items such as guavas, mangos, and avocados have stronger cultural connections to the people who live in places where these foods grow. Fresh food is also a naturally growing resource in these places. Another factor that falls under our ecological environment is population density. Is the environment homogeneous or diverse? Is it urban or rural? These factors produce cultural attributes associated within these spaces.

In a business, our environment includes the physical space in which we are invited to work, as in my example at the opening of this chapter. It can also be the size of the company, or whether it's digital, brick and mortar, or hybrid. It can even be the temperature in a conference room or whether or not there is access to coffee and snacks.

The factors that produce culture relate to our biology, evolution, and humanness and are described by psychologists David Matsumoto and Linda Juang as "the evolved human mind." This is basically a set of realities that include our human needs and motivations, our ability to adapt and evolve, our emotional capabilities, our basic needs to eat, sleep, and reproduce, and also include how we cope with disease and illness.

All of these factors impact business cultures. Just in the last eighteen months of this writing, business culture has had to shift dramatically because of a global pandemic. Our biological realities and need to keep ourselves and each other safe have pushed the boundaries of what many companies thought they could or couldn't do. Entire companies, school districts, and higher-education institutions transitioned to fully remote operations, which produced new cultural norms across their industries.

The outputs of each of these factors individually and collectively create what we identify as culture and include our language (words we use and how we use them), our beliefs (right/wrong, religion, our politics), our values (how we prioritize and place importance on one thing over another), traditions (cultural celebrations, milestones), norms (what we normalize as the "right" ways of being), and attitudes (opinions, biases, prejudices).

I'm sure you can think of many ways that these cultural attributes show up in your life, and how you may be a part of several communities with different cultures, or how parts of your cultural identity shine through more brilliantly when you are with different groups of people. For example, when you're hanging out with family and friends, you might use different words or have an accent that becomes more pronounced than when you're at work. Also, you may adhere to a set of norms or dress codes when you go to work that are different from your everyday ways of being.

> When you are creating a space, you are responsible for the culture that emerges from the space you create.

We all have the choice to be intentional about how we construct our environments so they facilitate how we want people to feel, to be, and to interact with each other. In equity-centered environments that are striving to be diverse, inclusive, equitable, and antiracist, we should want all members of the community to feel emotionally, psychologically, and physically safe; we want people to experience success; we want to be responsible stewards of power and privilege; and we want to equitably distribute resources.

Part of being intentional about space creation requires us to remember that despite all the intention and preparation we put into our space creation plan, people are not blank slates when they show up to work on the first day. People show up with years of prior learning, patterns, norms, and expectations that we've been taught elsewhere about what a work environment "should" be. It will take time to help people acclimate to this new environment, and one of the things that can help this process is to make sure that there is alignment between the three elements of your culture plan. For example, if you work in a warehouse with open floor plans and Ping-Pong tables, it might be difficult to get people to show up to work in formal suits and shoes. The space alone is enough to counter the messages of formal business practices. So, if you want to create a casual work environment, you need to create a casual physical space to support it, and vice versa. If you want a team to show up to a creative brainstorming session with a casual, fun energy, don't hold your session in a formal board-room. I know this might sound obvious, but trust me, it's not. When I was facilitating community equity work in inner-city school districts, it was almost impossible to convince a superintendent to come to a community center in casual dress to meet with parents even when they've said they wanted parents to feel comfortable attending school meetings, giving feedback, and being engaged. People with power are used to communicating that power in nonverbal ways and it can be difficult to break that pattern.

There have been other instances where I've met with executives of multimillion-dollar companies who show up on Zoom with a stale background (usually either a blank white wall behind them, or a fake image for their backdrop), leaning back in a chair, hands behind their heads, and talking to me while they are looking off the screen half of the time. I will not even take clients who show up like that because they are creating a space in which they are already "leaning out" of the process and are taking a casual approach to a situation where they have caused a lot of harm to Brown and Black folks in their communities. Executives I do work with come to consult, literally leaning in with their bodies, engaged, focused, and demonstrating real concern and commitment to the work ahead of them.

One of the biggest factors in workplace culture is in our social environment, so that's where we'll focus our attention for the remainder of this chapter. One of the first tasks clients do in our programs is to start thinking about how we create the policies and practices that will facilitate the healthy, intentional culture they envision for their teams, as well as their expanded community of clients and customers.

COMMUNITY GUIDELINES

I propose a new rule. If you work with other humans, you must have a set of community guidelines that you share, through a formal process, with any human that you work with or who works with you. You must have a plan for being accountable to those guidelines, and a shared understanding of what accountability looks like. In fact, I suggest that you communicate these guidelines before people commit to joining the community, and that their ongoing participation in the community is contingent on them committing to uphold them.

> Community guidelines are a set of statements that communicate expectations for how everyone is to behave in a space.

They can also be used to outline expectations for how people should use the resources the community offers, communicate clear boundaries, and provide an indication for what should be done if rules are violated. If you're not familiar with these kinds of protocols, the best comparison is the Facebook Group rules you have to accept before you're admitted to the group, but in real life. We share these protocols with new members of the group in very intentional ways, regularly revisiting them to make sure everyone is on the same page and updating them as needed.

Community guidelines can be called a number of different things, such as ground rules, community agreements, rules of engagement, but we want to avoid calling them "policies" or "behavioral standards." These kinds of words tend to have punitive connotations and are assigned by authority figures who have decided how they want everyone to act. Community agreements, on the other hand, are typically developed collaboratively, or at the very least are open to modification, additions, or amendments by members of the community.

If you've ever attended a DEI training at work, or any HR training on communication or interpersonal relationships, you're probably familiar with some of the typical community guidelines. And if I had to put money on it, I'd bet that on more than one occasion you've sat in the room and rolled your eyes as a facilitator asked for suggestions on group agreements and your fellow colleagues raised their hands and offered concepts such as respect, openness, putting away technology, and "only one person should talk at a time." Or it might even be the case that the coworker sharing those ideas was you. Don't worry, it's okay. There's no judgment coming from me. At one point in my career as a young facilitator, I was the person asking for those suggestions and writing them on the chart paper that I'd stick on the walls with masking tape (and by the grace of Queen Beyoncé we now have sticky Post-it Note chart paper). Those generic community agreements create pretty generic group cultures; they feel flat, impersonal, and unembodied because they are words that we haven't built any content around in the space. What I learned over time is that creating community guidelines that feel uniquely relevant to the topic you're addressing, or the work environment you're in, contributes to building an intentional culture because people start to relate to the community guidelines differently and have a deeper connection to how they are relevant in supporting the work.

Here are some examples of guidelines that I've used in various settings in my work over the last few years:

▪ **Remember that we are sharing a learning environment, but we are all on different journeys.** This community guideline is meant to help people who are in a group, working toward a similar goal, understand that even though they are sharing a learning space and supporting each other, they should not compare their outcomes to one another because they are not all on the same journey. The cultural traits of competition and comparison can arise in certain situations, especially in business settings or among groups of people who are high achievers. This guideline is a reminder that the goals of the spaces I facilitate have different metrics for what success looks like.

◾ **Practice getting comfortable being uncomfortable.** This guideline reminds community members that growth comes on the other side of discomfort. Together, we can practice getting more comfortable with the feelings and emotions that discomfort brings. This is especially true when conflict arises, or when someone says or does something harmful. Often, the desire to make one person feel more comfortable with their mistakes only creates a culture in which that mistake isn't taken seriously. We don't need to demean or "punish" people when they have wronged, but we also all need to be okay with everyone being uncomfortable for a while as the appropriate conversations, understandings, and ultimate resolution are being determined.

◾ **Comfort and safety are different things.** In some spaces, it is useful to create community guidelines around how terms or expressions can be used. This guideline is to gather agreement from participants to consider if an experience they are having in the group is causing a feeling that is uncomfortable or unsafe. Discomfort is the experience of being in situations or conversations that are out of the ordinary and pushing what you believe to be normal or "right." Feeling unsafe, on the other hand, involves being in harm's way and at risk of physical, emotional, or another form of injury (or reinjury) or lasting negative impact.

- ■ **"Yes, and . . ."** This is one of my favorite community guidelines, and also one of my personal life rules. It is a reminder that multiple experiences can be true at the same moment in time. They are equally real and valid experiences. When describing this agreement, I also mention that this is an invitation to use the word "but" very intentionally. Oftentimes, we use the word "but" as a way to defend our perspective, experience, or intent and, in the process, we dismiss the perspectives, experiences, and intentions of others. For example, "I understand that it's stressful to be a stay-at-home parent, but working parents have really stressful lives too." The use of "but" in this statement is a defense against the idea that stay-at-home parents have as much or more stress than working parents, even though they started the sentence with the statement "I understand." The truth is that both parents experience high levels of stress. If this person used the work and, instead of but, offered: "I understand that it's stressful to be a stay-at-home parent, and working parents have really stressful lives too," they'd be communicating the sentiment that both experiences are true.

- ■ **People are experts in their own lives.** This agreement places an emphasis on lived experiences and centers the experiences of people who are most impacted by an issue. I might be an expert in diversity, equity, and inclusion, but I do not know more about a person's life or experiences than any singular person living their own life in their own community.

This leads me to my favorite community agreement and rule for life:

■ **It depends.** As a community agreement, this phrase is a reminder that in equity work there is not always one perfect answer that applies to every business, issue, inequity, or dilemma that arises. I know we live in a world that likes to sort things into binaries: Good/Bad, Black/White, Fair/Unfair. But the truth is that life is more nuanced. The short answer to most things is "it depends," and we need to be willing to have discussions, think about our values, and consider multiple perspectives in order to come to a conclusion about how to move forward.

My invitation to you is to create community agreements that are specific for your space and that reflect the culture you're cultivating. Be prepared to talk about each of your guidelines within the context of your community, how they relate to the work ahead, and why it's important to maintain the safety of the group. Be willing to have different guidelines for different settings within your community. For example, a guideline like, "Remember that we are sharing a learning environment, but we are all on different journeys," might not be suitable if the group is formed to accomplish a very concrete goal or become competent in a highly specific skill. Although it might still be true that "we are all on different journeys," this may feel like gaslighting to folks who have shown up to achieve a very concrete goal wherein success is not subjective. Other guidelines might be better suited for short-term groups over long-term groups, or teams of coworkers might require different agreements than a group of program participants or clients.

I also invite you to consider the creation of your guidelines as a collaborative process. As the space creator, always prepare to show up with clear guidelines that you have for the group and always ask if others have more to add, or questions or feedback about the guidelines being proposed.

Once you've created the guidelines and gotten feedback, then you have to get participant agreement. In our Institute for Equity-Centered Coaching, our students sign off on community agreements after they've participated in an orientation session that we facilitate for each new cohort. The agreement says that they understand the agreements, agree to follow them, and recognize that if they do not follow them, there will be a process to address any violation or harm. And then there is an expectation of accountability and repair.

ACCOUNTABILITY AND REPAIR

One of the hardest parts of creating space is holding people accountable and facilitating repair, especially if the person in power is the one who has violated the community's values or community guidelines. I really hope you're on board, because what I have to say here might feel uncomfortable.

Leaders are capable of violating their own values and commitments. Sometimes this is unintentional, and sometimes leaders do it knowing that they are out of alignment. And sometimes they do it anyway, because they can. If this feels like I'm talking about you, or about someone you know, I'm not . . . not yet, anyway. In the last twelve months alone, there have been numerous companies and influencers whose actions have violated their own standards or values. In fact, it happens so frequently that I don't even have to name a single person or company before you start to think of brands that fit this description. But just in case you need an example: In 2021, Rachel Hollis, a multimillionaire entrepreneur and influencer, who built a brand off of "small-town girl" vibes and "If I can do it, anyone can" mantras, released a series of TikTok videos in which she referred to her domestic aide as "the woman who cleans her toilets." Hollis went on to describe how she works hard for her privileges and that not everyone is willing to work as hard as she does, and ultimately closed her video with the messages "What makes you think I want to be relatable? If I'm relatable, I'm doing it wrong." The backlash was immediate and went on for days, followed by a series of non-apologies from Hollis deflecting and blaming her team, while never actually taking responsibility for what she said. Instead, she merely demonstrated a complete lack of understanding of why the things she said were inappropriate and were a huge deviation from her brand.

But this, dear reader, is about you (unless you happen to be Rachel Hollis, in which case . . . girl, give me a call). This is about your ability to be self-reflective and aligned because your community is a reflection of you. You are establishing the culture and standards for your team, as well as for your customers, clients, and community members. If you have leadership teams, you are establishing a culture within them, which trickles down to everyone else with whom they interact. Remember that human relationships are the core aspect of a culture's DNA. Accountability starts with you. How do you show up when you've made a mistake? Can you accept and incorporate critical feedback? Are there retaliatory consequences when there is a conflict? Is your leadership liberatory or oppressive?

And obviously, as evidenced by the example above, you can make hella money by conducting yourself in oppressive, unaligned, inequitable ways. But that is not antiracist practice. That is not how you show up in your leadership if you are committed to diversity, equity, and inclusion (more on leadership in Chapter 9).

Now that we've covered your personal responsibility in setting the tone through your own actions, we can explore how we establish accountability within our communities. You'll have to learn how to be comfortable with managing conflict and facilitating processes for accountability and repair. Part of your space-creation planning should include creating clear definitions for what accountability in your community looks like so that everyone understands what would occur if there were a violation of the agreements, or if someone were to behave in ways that are inconsistent with the community values.

The following is a framework for accountability that you can use as a starting point for your own practice:

1. A call for accountability is made.

   This can be done by the person(s) harmed, or it can come from an advocate or activist who is speaking in support of the harmed community member.

2. The person who has caused harm or made a mistake takes ownership.

   This is the point where the person takes accountability. They own what they've done.

3. The person who takes accountability reaches out to the person or community who was harmed and makes themselves available to the person they have harmed and talks with them if that is desired.

   This is the point at which some folks choose to bring in a skilled facilitator to mediate or support the discussion that needs to take place. Professional facilitators will create boundaries for the discussion, ensure that the conversation doesn't get derailed, and support both parties equitably to ensure a productive conversation that leaves all parties feeling restored or transformed by the process.

4. The person who takes accountability then carries out the reparative actions that the harmed person or persons have requested to the extent that this is possible.

   At this point, the person who takes accountability takes whatever actions have been agreed upon. A facilitator can help the parties come to an agreement on what repair or transformation looks like. Sometimes, the harmed party wants an action that can't be taken because of real constraints, or even boundaries that the other party has. For example, if I want a person to provide monetary compensation that is beyond their means, they have the right to decline and offer another solution.

5. There is a public sharing of the progress unless the harmed person has requested otherwise.

In many accountability processes, there will be a public account of what happened, and the person taking responsibility will own their full participation and share whatever they can about the actions taken to ensure that the issue does not happen again. However, some people who have been harmed do not want a public account to take place because they would like to move on. They have the right to their privacy.

6. The person who takes accountability stops the action or behavior or permanently changes a policy or procedure that caused the harm. Ideally, this person becomes an advocate for long-term change.

What I want to point out about this framework is that it is one example, and not the only framework that exists. What's most important is that all the parties are consenting to the process at each step, and that there is a shared understanding of expectations throughout the process.

A lot of conflict arises just because people have different expectations for how other people should respond.

Taking the time to get on the same page, define what we mean, be clear about what we think accountability should look like, and ultimately stay focused on the person or people who have experienced harm are ways to keep the process moving forward.

DIVERSITY, EQUITY, AND EXPLICIT INCLUSION

The points we'll explore around this theme of creating space are really about the concepts of inclusion and accessibility. Inclusion is the act of including others with policies, procedures, and practices. It's all of the things you do to help people feel welcomed and included in a space. Because your values also call for you to create spaces that are diverse, creating spaces that are inclusive is a must if you want to ensure that people are having equitable experiences. That is the formula of diversity, equity, and inclusion.

If you want to have the best business outcomes, and you want your business to be a leader in creating positive social impact, you need a diverse community. The more diversity you have, the more inclusion you need to facilitate in order to achieve equitable outcomes. This is done through antiracist practice. Unfortunately, we are truly just at the start of employing antiracist practices in the workplace and in how we train and discuss diversity within the workforce.

According to a 2007 article, "History of Diversity Training and Its Pioneers," in *Diversity Officer Magazine*, the emphasis on racial diversity took a back seat to gender equity throughout the 1970s and '80s, and then throughout the '90s diversity expanded its efforts to include different marginalized groups, such as gay and lesbian diversity, age diversity (primarily concerned with including millennials who were entering the workforce and who had important contributions to make), religious diversity, and ability diversity. In the places where racial diversity work was happening, like the

United States Department of Defense (rolling emoji eyes), the military found that, after attending diversity trainings, participants fell into one of three groups: 1) becoming more insightful about race relations, 2) becoming more resistant to racial harmony, and 3) becoming "what the military referred to as 'fanatics', defined as 'advocating for any instance of racial injustice after the training.'"[1]

By the time I started my career as a Diversity Trainer in 2008, the work was being couched in anti-bullying work, interpersonal relations, and moving people from being a bystander to being an ally for any sort of discrimination, harassment, or prejudicial behavior. It was basically compliance work and did not directly address racism. It wasn't until I started my own consulting firm in 2013 that I was able to openly name in workshops the impacts of interpersonal and institutional racism, White privilege, and White supremacy without being afraid of being fired from a job (and that's only because I was my own boss).

This seems like the equivalent to a gynecologist not being able to say the word "vagina" with their patients. That's what it felt like to have been a DEI consultant up through 2018, and even in some spaces today it's still not easy to say all the words you need to use in order to adequately address the issues.

Inclusion and equity, and now antiracism, have to be included in the conversation if we are going to get anywhere, because diversity is not enough. As a space creator, you need to understand this. If you are focused on creating diversity without inclusion, you are likely to tokenize people, or fail to give them an equitable experience. This is like throwing a party and inviting a wide variety of people to come and enjoy brunch on your rooftop balcony, but when the guests arrive, some of them can't eat half the food because you didn't consider allergies or dietary restrictions, and since the building didn't have an elevator, some of the folks on your invite list couldn't get to the party because they can't access the roof.

For years now I've been teaching a concept I call "explicit inclusion." I use this term because, in businesses that are seeking to be antiracist, sometimes you actually won't be including everyone, even though you are bringing together a broad diversity of people. To protect the safety of some folks, you might have to exclude others. For example, if you run a business that prioritizes travel for Black and Brown folks, it would be critical for you to not welcome people who hold explicit anti-Black sentiments. If you run an Asian grocery store, you should have every right to not be inclusive of people who have anti-Asian views. And if you have a core belief that #BlackLivesMatter, it may not be a safe space if you are also welcoming police.

One example of this is a small, local, worker-owned coffee shop and radical bookstore, Hasta Muerte Coffee, in Oakland, California. If you go to their website, the first thing you'll see is the company's commitment statement: "We are committed to nurturing community while serving the best coffee, hasta la muerte. Offering drinks and snacks and hosting a specialty bookstore, we hope to provide a warm and inclusive atmosphere."

In 2018, the Hasta Muerte Coffee gained national attention from national news outlets for enforcing their policy of not serving police officers. The worker-owners came to this conclusion by engaging in dialogue with each other and their community and realized that the community they were serving had a history of negative interactions with police and that police officers' presence in their establishment would be inconsistent with their commitment to a warm, inclusive environment for their community. Worker-owners not only created a community guideline and policy about not serving police, but they also had a plan for communicating the policy, and a procedure detailing exactly what any worker would say to a police officer if they entered the establishment.[2] (Note: In May 2021, Hasta Muerte Coffee released a booklet titled "No Abolition Without Autonomy" that provides more details about the case for antiracist participation for small businesses and details about the incident that sparked the national attention they received. You can go to their website to download the booklet, or you can find it on this book's online resource page.)

This part of space creation, explicit inclusion, asks us to take the time to truly consider the needs of our communities that will ultimately facilitate their success. Consider asking the following questions:

- What does our staff need to help them feel like they have all the resources to do their jobs effectively?
- What do they need that will help them understand that we are an antiracist business, and they can begin to release the harmful patterns they've picked up in toxic work environments?
- Where do I host my retreats? Are they inclusive to nonbinary people? Are there gender-neutral bathrooms?
- Is my conference lineup reflective of the community I want to gather for this event?
- What accessibility accommodations do I need in place to make sure that colleagues, clients, and customers can access products or services if they are differently abled?

Ask these kinds of questions now. If you have not yet started your business or are just starting, that's great. If you've been around for a while and are making boatloads of money, now's a great time to start asking these questions too. Anywhere you fall in the journey, it's never too early to be in this inquiry, and this is a mode of inquiry that doesn't stop. As you grow deeper into your antiracist practice, you'll consider more ways to be inclusive, and over time your own understanding of equity will shift and expand as you incorporate new learnings into your commitments. And with each decision you make to be more inclusive to those at the margins, you contribute to bending the arc of the moral universe a little more swiftly.

CHAPTER 8

MAKE FRIENDS WITH MONEY

In 2016, after I'd been growing my consulting side-hustle, while still working full-time in various nonprofits, I was at the point where I needed to either press the gas and go all-in in my business or accept that I'd spend the rest of my career in nonprofit and educational institutions, hoping that I'd be able to retire one day in the future. I started looking for a next-level business training and so I applied, and was accepted, to be a part of a business incubator for social entrepreneurs. The program provided training and mentorship to business owners who wanted to focus on building businesses that would create some sort of positive social or environmental impact, in addition to being financially successful.

I learned a lot about business from this program, but the most transformative lessons were so obvious, they were comical. We were about midway through the program, where cohort members would spend one long weekend a month in intensive training with one month of integration between sessions, and during this particular session I was meeting with one of the business mentors to present my business model and projected budget. The mentor looked very carefully at the budget and said, "Trudi, this is a great business model, but why does your budget end in zero?"

I seriously could not even process the question. I was thinking to myself, "What do you mean, 'Why does the budget end in zero'? Why wouldn't it?" The mentor must have been able to tell that I was confused because of my lack of response, and followed by pointing at the spreadsheet and saying, "You're projecting to earn all this money, but in your expenses, you've spent everything you've earned. You're not planning to make a profit?" And just like that, I could see. It was like the words somehow dissolved a pair of dirty-ass, nonprofit shades that I had been wearing for years that I hadn't even realized were clouding my view.

At that point in my life, I had spent almost fifteen years learning to build and maximize budgets for nonprofits where not spending all the money you were given was a liability. If you got a grant for $50,000 and you spent $40,000 you would be sending a check back to the funder for the difference, and giving back money would put future funding opportunities in jeopardy. When you apply for a grant, you have to tell the funder exactly how you will use every dollar, so ending up with money at the end of the funding cycle means you didn't execute your plan. I had managed private, public, and even federal grants programs worth millions of dollars and so it hadn't occurred to me to build a business plan that left me with a profit. This is one the symptoms of what I have come to call "nonprofit mindset syndrome."

> Nonprofit mindset syndrome is a set of beliefs that are perpetuated by nonprofits and public service organizations, including schools, libraries, and much of the human service sector, that trains professionals in these industries to accept the conditions of scarcity of resources.

Through this mindset, we are indoctrinated to believe that if one person gains, another person loses, and that we should feel so grateful for every penny we do earn, because others have it so much harder (yes, this is true, and yet, I will explain below how this is also harmful). The shitty part is that you have to adopt a nonprofit mindset to function in this sector, earning less than you need to thrive and, if you're lucky, you're no more than a few paychecks away from broke.

Nonprofit mindset isn't the only thing I was battling against. I was also doing my best to fight against the psychological stress of poverty. At that point I'd been on various forms of social service aid over the course of my life, on and off of food stamps a few times, evicted once, and living with the trauma of losing my childhood home. Even though I had dreams of being rich, I clearly didn't know how to make that happen.

This isn't something that is unique to me. After working with hundreds of people who want to start impact-driven businesses, I've seen the pattern of entrepreneurs who come from human service professions, or social justice activism, who have very conflicted feelings about their real need to generate revenue, the desire to live the life of their dreams, and a deep calling to solve problems affecting people and communities that don't have the resources to pay for services. And it's not just from people who grew up poor, or nonprofit professionals who adopt nonprofit, or no-profit mindsets. I've worked with people who grew up with money, in some cases extreme wealth, who have taken a life path where they are committed to improving the world for others, and they, too, develop a conflicted relationship with their own generational wealth. But none of these feelings will help us pursue our antiracist goals.

Let's remember that the ultimate goals of antiracism are equity and freedom. That we no longer live in a world where neither our race nor our zip code is a determinant of our life outcomes. That people have the ability to pursue whatever life they want and have the same access to opportunities and success as anyone else. Antiracist practice is not about making anyone a martyr to the movement and resigning themselves to a life of poverty because we've bought into the idea that money is bad, and capitalism is bad, and money changes people. That will not lead us to an equitable world.

There will have to be a lot of effort and innovation to achieve the type of ultimate liberation that antiracist activists are working toward, and if we think that we will get there without a reimagined relationship to money, we are simply out of touch. I'm not saying that we all need to be millionaires. That is not everyone's goal, and not every entrepreneur wants to put that kind of pressure on their business or themselves. And we shouldn't have to. What I am saying is that we need to make friends with money so that those of us who are contributing to building an antiracist society can also build sustainable healthy businesses, create jobs, pay people equitably, make financial contributions to efforts that will advance our antiracist goals, and also enjoy what the world has to offer us.

SOMEONE'S GOTTA FUND THE MOVEMENT

Antiracism efforts exist at the intersections of racism and every other tool that society has used to oppress people. Gender equity, educational equity, health equity, housing equity, and equity related to justice reform and the prison industrial complex are just a few of the areas of concern that antiracist activists are working on, and all of them require time, political will, and money to advance those efforts.

It is in our best interest that we antiracist practitioners, accomplices, and allies lean into the possibilities and privileges that

134 ■ THE ANTIRACIST BUSINESS BOOK

wealth building affords us. We can be responsible stewards of the wealth we create and fund efforts for radical change in industries and movements that do not have their own inherent funding streams, including supporting political candidates that will advance antiracist policy, investing in businesses that are pursing equity and decolonization practices, building new educational institutions that use liberated teaching and learning models, and so much more. When we reframe our relationship to money, as antiracist entrepreneurs, moving beyond "Money is a necessary evil that I have to learn to deal with" to "Money is a resource that can be leveraged for good, and I am comfortable and confident in my ability to earn, manage, and leverage it," we increase our capacity to make an impact beyond our own lives and businesses.

HOW MONEY MINDSET AND UNCONSCIOUS BIAS WORK ARE LINKED

I'm not gonna lie to you. The first time I ever heard someone tell me that I needed to work on my money mindset, I crossed my arms, rolled my eyes, and stopped listening. I definitely was not trying to hear some random White lady, who just told me she grew up wealthy, tell me that I wasn't attracting money into my life because my money mindset was jacked up. Then she sold me a coaching service that was going to reprogram my brain to be more accepting of money. Yes, I bought the course, because, as I said in the first chapter of this book, I was at the point where I felt like these White folks had figured something out that I hadn't, and I was at least willing to see what the hell they were talking about. But this is not the story where I tell you that the program changed my money mindset and I made a million dollars in six weeks. I actually found the program to be very gaslighting, slightly traumatic, and I couldn't finish it. It was this experience that fueled my commitment to creating more culturally responsive approaches to coaching, and my desire to ultimately train coaches to provide services that were equity-centered and antiracist. What this program did do, however, was set me on a path to realize how a money mindset was another equity issue that needed to be addressed.

While I was coping with the emotional toll this experience had taken on me, I was working on my PhD and spending a lot of time sitting with ecological human development theory, which basically tells us that people are a product of a variety of systems and environments they encounter throughout their lives from the moment they are born. These systems include our nuclear family, extended family, neighborhoods, school communities, and various institutions we interact with including churches, community centers, and media outlets (TV shows, radio, games, social media). We are taught things both explicitly, through formal instruction, and implicitly, just by watching the world around us and learning its unwritten rules for what is right and wrong.

It is through these mechanisms that bias, prejudice, and discrimination are perpetuated and internalized. I realized that if I already believed that we pick up preferences, biases, beliefs, and prejudices from our environments and that those biases, beliefs, and prejudices result in conscious and unconscious discriminatory behavior, and impact our relationships with people every day, then that same logic can be applied to money.

> We learn things about money, wealth, and poverty both implicitly and explicitly through our environments that result in certain biases, beliefs, emotions, and prejudices about money that lead to a variety of behavioral patterns.

If we allow our implicit biases affect our decision making and behavior around every other choice in our lives, how could they not affect how we earn or fail to earn money?

MONEY MINDSET ANTI-HACKS FOR NEW ENTREPRENEURS

Money mindset work isn't just some New Age, law of attraction trend. It's actually culture work, antibias work, and part of a self-awareness practice that is tied to our personal liberation. And although I can't provide you with any quick tricks or hacks to immediately change your relationship to money, I can give you some tips to practice over time.

- **Make actual friends with people who have money.** Seriously, this is a game changer. If you can start networking with people who are making more money than you, you'll start to notice mindset differences and small lifestyle differences that, over time, will start to rub off on you. And I'm not suggesting that you fake relationships or that you position yourself to be able to take advantage of them in a manipulative way. I'm talking about being open to making friends with people who have varying lifestyles and backgrounds so that you can start to expand your awareness about the different relationships people have with money. If you grew up broke, and you stay broke, and all your friends are broke, you're in an echo chamber related to your community's relationship with money. By meeting people with different relationships to money, you start to pull away from that echo chamber and start to see alternative ways of being. Some of them you might disagree with, while others you might actually like and want to incorporate into your life.

■ **Get familiar with what you've already invested.** Start paying attention to the effort that you put into your work. Consider, for a moment, how many years of your life you've spent building your expertise, learning a skill, and purchasing materials to practice making your wares. Think about all those nights you spend with YouTube on your phone, and your computer on your lap learning and simultaneously doing at the same time. How many hours have you fiddled around in Canva making a template for your slides, or creating a graphic to share in Instagram? Who paid you for that?

Getting familiar with what things cost in time, energy, and actual money will start to show you how much you've already invested in yourself and your business. Even if those investments didn't result in tangible outcomes, you hold the cumulative knowledge and experience of everything you've ever done. Now that you're putting all of that expertise into your business to sell something, how much did it cost you to be able to produce? And what do you need to be compensated in order to feel like there has been an equitable exchange?

■ **Find your freedom number.** Your freedom number is the amount of money you would need to earn every month in order to pay your bills, build up your savings, and be able to live the life that you want to live. The great thing about a freedom number is that it's different for everyone. Some people want to go off the grid and live in a tiny house and they don't need a large recurring monthly income to pay for their life. For others, the number is higher because the way they want to live requires more income. There shouldn't be a judgment on what's better or worse. Finding our freedom number lets us calibrate our dreams with our earnings. We have every right to change the version of our life that we want at any given time.

- **Play with the numbers.** Once you have your freedom number, start playing with numbers to see what you would have to do to hit your freedom number. For example, if your freedom number is $100,000 before taxes, you can figure out how many units of your product or service you need to sell to get there, and then you get to decide if that feels aligned. You can sell ten consulting plans at $10k, you can sell twenty at $5k, or you can sell one hundred units of something that costs $1,000.

  I am intentionally using the word "play" because I really want this to be a fun, imaginative exercise instead of something that feels tense and stressful. Imagine if you had $1,000,000 to start a company. What would you build? Who would you hire? How much would you pay them? How much would you put into marketing? Where would your office be? Have fun with what the future can bring. You'll be surprised at how much easier it can be to actually create it.

  This exercise is probably the one that has had the most profound impact on me, other than making friends with people who have money. It opens up your imagination and gives you permission to see what's possible, in addition to helping you to calibrate your mind and nervous system to think about larger amounts of money than you might be used to. If that seems too overwhelming, start the exercise using $250k or even $100k as the starting number and see what you can dream up.

- **Build the life you want, while you're living the life you have.** For years, I'd been listening to people tell me about all the things they'll do . . . one day. One day, when I retire . . . One day, when I finish school . . . One day, when my kids are grown . . . One day, when I hit the lotto . . . I was terrified of living my life for "one day" in the future. Maybe it was because I didn't have any real evidence that "one day" would ever come. Something about this scared me because my dreams were so big and urgent that they couldn't wait. I wasn't willing to wait until my kids were grown before I started to travel. I wasn't willing to wait until school to start my business. I couldn't imagine a reality where I was waiting for my life to start; meanwhile, time was just flying by me.

Imagine that you are standing at the edge of a lake, and out in the middle of the lake is a future version of your life where you get to have everything you want. Imagine that there is a long rope tied to that future life of yours, and the rope extends across the water and onto the shore. You have some choices. You can pick up the rope, stand at the shore, and pull the rope until eventually your future life reaches you at the shore, or you can pull the rope while you're taking steps toward it, and eventually you will meet your future somewhere in the middle.

This second version of pulling your future toward you, while you are also moving toward it, is an invitation to build your future and experience joy and pleasure at the same time. Do this by celebrating your wins, giving yourself permission to splurge on a fancy dinner or nice outfit, go on vacation, or even just take a weekday off and spend the day at the beach. Do something that feels like a luxury. You're already working hard enough to build a responsible, antiracist business and managing the rest of your life. Give yourself permission to use some of the money you are earning, and invest in things and experiences that bring you joy.

EQUITY-CENTERED PRICING AND SALES

Now that we've made the case for why you need to get comfortable with money and we've addressed some of the mindset challenges you may be facing, let's talk about how we actually make money. Sales.

If we're not selling something, are we even in business? No, we are not. Getting comfortable with marketing and sales is a nonnegotiable part of the plan if we're going to create an antiracist business, but we need to approach the sales and marketing part of our practice with just as much intention as the rest of our work. It's really easy to fall into oppressive, manipulative, misaligned tactics in our sales and marketing process, because sales and marketing advice is so easy to come by, and many entrepreneurs are so focused on scaling that we forget to apply our equity lens to this aspect of our business.

It's important to remember that equity-centered sales is not about increasing the diversity of your audience. I've been in very awkward conversations with people who ask me if they should offer scholarships or discounts to programs or products in order to make it more "accessible" or to increase diversity among their clientele. This question is rooted in an assumption that the reason they don't have a diverse audience, or diverse clientele, is due to unaffordability. This is an inherently racist assumption connected to the stereotype that Black and Brown folks don't have money to afford your services. It's also a bit egotistical, because the alternative side of this assumption is that if Black and Brown people had more money, they'd want to spend it with your company. The fact is that there are plenty of people of all races and ethnicities who can afford your service. The questions become: 1) Are those people in your audience, and are you marketing to those people? 2) Do those people want to patronize your business?

> Scholarships, discounts, and sliding scales can all be components of an equity-based strategy, but this isn't the first place you start. You have to make sure that your business is healthy in the first place. Which means you need a plan for selling your products and services, paying yourself and your business expenses, and making a profit.

There's a lot of advice out there that will tell you to just pick a number that you feel comfortable with, then double it, or triple it. There's also a bit of gaslighting that takes place among business coaches who tell their clients that if they can't double or triple their rates, there's something wrong with their self-worth or their mindset. This is a major oversimplification of the process in determining your rates, and of the selling process. This is emotional stuff, especially if you're in business for the purpose of some larger-scale change that you hope to create in the world. The advice to double or triple your rates is arbitrary, and not equity-centered.

The following is an approach to coming up with the cost of your products and services that is anchored in actual data and the realities of your personal and business context. My hope for you is that you can come up with a pricing structure that feels aligned with your needs and your goals so that you don't feel like you're throwing spaghetti at a wall or pulling numbers out of thin air.

- ▪ **Determine direct costs of offering the program, product, or service.** What is this actually going to cost to deliver? Figure out the hourly rates of your team members and your own time. Think about how long they will work while delivering the actual service and the time it takes to prepare to deliver it. It's easy to forget about the time you spend designing something, building, and testing it, and even responding to clients and customers who have questions about it. Calculate the cost of any supplies you need to buy, software you'll use, money to brand the product, and any other cost associated with developing and implementing the thing that you're selling.

■ **What are the indirect costs?** Indirect costs are any expenses not directly associated with creating or delivering the product or service. This could include salaries for staff that are not directly implementing services or making products (marketing team, office assistants, etc.), rent for your physical company space, utility bills, health benefits. Typically, companies can come up with a percentage of the overall budget that you add to all revenue streams to account for these costs.

■ **How much money will be invested in marketing?** Your marketing costs can include things like paid ads, and costs associated with hiring team members, such as copywriters, graphic designers, and photographers, to support the marketing campaign. Your direct costs, indirect costs, and marketing expenses represent the hard cost of your product or service. It's what you'll need to make in order to break even. If you are a nonprofit or no-profit business, you can stop here. But if you're actually interested in making money that can be used to grow your business, pay out bonuses, hire new people, donate to causes, or do something fabulous for yourself, you need to move to the next step.

■ **Determine your desired profit margin and anticipated taxes.** How much do you want or need to make in order to continue to grow? What do you need to make to feel like you're making progress according to your own version of success? Although what qualifies as a "good" profit margin differs across industries, it is generally accepted that anything over 20 percent of your total costs is a good or healthy profit margin. You also want to add a line for your anticipated taxes, and you should work with your accountant to determine what percentage of your revenue you should be putting aside for this.

Let's do the math:

Direct cost: $10,000
Indirect costs: $3,500
Marketing costs: $1,000
Profit: $5,000
Taxes: $5,850

Total revenue goal: $25,350

Now that you have a goal for your product or service that will allow you to cover your costs, pay yourself, pay your taxes, and leave some money in the bank that you can reinvest in your business or impact initiatives, you can start to reverse engineer the cost of your product or service.

Let's say you're running a group program for twelve people. One option is to simply split the total revenue goal across the number of people you will serve. In this case, the individual cost would be around $2,113 per person (I would probably round up to $2,220). If you're selling a product and you have one hundred units of the product to sell, you know you have to price the product at $253.50. If you have one thousand units, the cost per unit is $25.35.

This process is meant both to help you understand what your actual costs are and give you a pricing strategy that is directly related to your business model and goals. You can always charge more, you can increase the amount of profit you'd like to make, and you can lower your costs elsewhere, but you can't go below your minimum revenue goal if you want to have a sustainable business.

WHAT MAKES THIS AN EQUITY-CENTERED STRATEGY?

Although this strategy has nothing to do with identity (which has been overly correlated to the term "equity" over the last few years), it has everything to do with equity. Equity is about ensuring that people have what they need to thrive and grow, which means that some people get different types of support in order to achieve the same goals. Anchoring our pricing strategy in actual costs helps us keep our own money mindset in check when we want to start slashing prices or offering discounts. If we're not making arbitrary decisions about costs, it's easier to stand firm in our choices, and to remember that our business needs must be accounted for. It is inequitable to you, as an entrepreneur, to work all night and not pay yourself just as it's inequitable for a pharmaceutical company to increase the cost of Daraprim, a lifesaving drug that went from $13.50 to $750 overnight (looking at you, Turing Pharmaceuticals).

GETTING YOUR PRODUCTS OR SERVICES SOLD

There are many ways to sell your products and services. You can sell them in a store, on a web page, through various vendors, in person, and even on the phone. There are actually too many ways to sell for us to explore here. However, I would be negligent if I didn't take some time to talk about some dos and don'ts as far as your sales process is concerned, especially since so many of the folks we work with share stories about how their sales processes have gone wrong, and especially how harm and microaggressions have occurred in these sales processes. Here are the three most important things to remember when it comes to being equitable in your sales:

1. **Be Honest and Clear.** Tell people who your target audience is. Tell them real outcomes that they can expect and give them an idea about what they should not expect from your product or service. Too often, people are selling a dream and positioning their best, most rare examples of success as a highlight to what is possible. This can be manipulative, especially if you're coupling these tactics with no-return/no-refund policies.

2. **Don't Use Shame as a Sales Tool.** When salespeople ask clients if they are scared to make an investment or tell them that their hesitation to purchase is a character flaw or mindset issue, they are participating in gaslighting and manipulation. This is done so often because it's effective. Yes, people will buy, but it is an exploitation of power because the salesperson is seen as someone who has a solution to a problem the client has or a barrier between where the client is now and where they want to be. For example, if I go to a car dealership and I drive an old Honda Civic and I want to be in a new 6-series BMW, the salesperson is trying to make the bridge between my current, Civic-driving self and the potential future 6-series-driving version of myself. All I have to do is listen to the salesperson who is telling me that they can put me in this car, even if I actually can't afford the monthly payments. The salesperson holds the power to transform us into the person we envision ourselves to be. Using shame to sell is an exploitation of that power.

   I can hear the critics now. "No one can 'make' you buy anything," and "What about personal responsibility?" But if salespeople and markets don't have the upper hand in these situations, then why do people study sales and marketing psychology? There is an entire field of study that examines the way our brains and emotions work when we are making purchases, and this information is often used to create intentional conditions that optimize the chances that someone will purchase something. Which means that unless the customer is armed with the exact same information about sales psychology as the salesperson, they are at a disadvantage. This means that the salesperson has more power. Free will and personal responsibility are not ethical arguments to defend manipulation, exploitation, and abuse of power.

3. **Give People Time to Think.** When we rush people to make decisions, we increase the chances that they will regret their decision. Even though urgency is a real motivator, we don't need to create fake urgency by making things up like, "This is your last chance to buy," or "We only have two seats left," if those things are not true. If they are true, then the urgency is real. For example, the Institute for Equity-Centered Coaching has a firm start date for each starting class. If you miss the deadline, you can't start late. That is not fake urgency—it's a real constraint that has to do with the integrity of the program. If you have five items left in your inventory, then that's a real urgency that you can communicate and encourage people to act on. But when we are faking urgency, people catch on and your brand can be seen as dishonest. If someone needs time to think or to talk to a spouse before making a decision, let them.

And please don't take this to mean you shouldn't follow up with people or support them in their purchasing decision. Some people need that. But you should get consent to follow up, and when they give you a "No, not interested," honor that no. It might be a "No, not right now," in which case, they'll stick around in your community, and they'll be back if and when they are ready.

Our relationships to money can be very complicated, and they are not going to get uncomplicated easily. But as with any other area of our life and personal growth that feels uncomfortable, we need to lean into these conversations if we are going to change our relationship to money and wealth. And, quite frankly, any widespread equity advancement that we are envisioning is going to require monetary investments to be made.

> Whether we are talking about racial equity, housing, health, food access, education, or overall quality of life, we won't get there without leaders investing in these movements within their local communities.

I recently shared a post on Instagram that stated that I am working on a five-million-dollar revenue plan for 2022. Ten years ago, I probably couldn't have even said that number out loud and taken myself seriously. It was too big. My mind couldn't even wrap my head around how much money that actually is, never mind building a plan to earn it in a year. Over the years, I've had to do all of the things I've just shared with you. When I was transitioning out of full-time employment, my goals were to simply make enough money in my business to pay my basic bills, then I needed to replace my income, then I started to upgrade my life. I bought an Infinity and moved from an apartment over a pizza shop into a small house that I rented from a friend, and last year I bought one of my dream homes. I don't need to grow my business to five million dollars next year, or any year, in order to sustain my life. But if I don't, here are some of the things that I feel deeply called to do that I cannot do unless I expand to my fullest potential:

- Open an (un)school. Opening a nontraditional unschooling center in Hartford, CT, that is free or low-cost to families has been a dream of mine for years. The impact that this could have on families and kids who need alternatives to public school would be profound.
- Invest in other companies that have antiracist business and liberatory leadership practices. Companies that create jobs that pay equitable, living wages, and honor people's humanity.
- Create a scholarship fund for teen/young parents who want to pursue higher education but have barriers to childcare, technology, and mentorship.
- Purchase homes, rehab them, and then sell them to families who need non-exploitative lease-to-own options to make homeownership more accessible to families.

This is not everyone's path. It's actually quite a stressful one to take. But I truly believe it is my purpose and that if I have the vision to do these things, and the capacity to make them happen, then it's actually more than just a dream—it's a responsibility. I believe that there are more people like me who have a feeling in their gut about their purpose. You will get there, but it will require a major leveling up of your mindset, your relationship to money, and your faith in yourself. You got this.

PART 3

LIBERATORY LEADERSHIP

Leadership is about empathy. It is about having the ability to relate to and connect with people for the purpose of inspiring and empowering their lives.

OPRAH WINFREY

CHAPTER 9

BUILDING AN ANTIRACIST TEAM

In 2011 (when I realized that I couldn't continue working in the leaky high school basement), I applied for a position that was my dream job at the time. It was for a director gig at a community school with a large community-based agency that was primarily known for providing therapeutic services to children and families. In addition to providing mental health services, the organization had a presence inside a number of the district public schools providing clinical mental health services as well as youth development programs. In case you're not familiar with community schools, these are public schools that partner with a nonprofit as the school's lead agency, and the lead agency is responsible for coordinating wraparound services with the children in that school and with the wider community. In some community schools, the school is treated as a hub for community services and is open from early in the morning until later in the evening, providing adult education services, health services, and community meetings.

I had just completed my master's degree when I saw the job posting for the position of a community school director. The person hired for the job would be responsible for building a team and rolling out an after-school program to serve about one hundred students and coordinating a number of other programs in the school. I applied immediately and quickly received an interview. There was just one potential problem. The job posting didn't have a salary range, and when I called to ask what the salary range was, I was told that their company policy prohibits them from sharing that information.

So, I figured I'd have to go to the interview and ask. But my situation was very clear to me. I couldn't make any less than I had currently been making (at $55,000 per year) in order to support my family of five. My partner and I decided that I would be the one to go back to work, since one of us needed to stay home to care for our toddler and manage the schedules of our two middle schoolers, and I'd invested the time and money into a degree that I was not only gainfully employed in, but also successful in moving up the nonprofit leadership ladder. It didn't make sense for both of us to work, so of course one of us had to sacrifice our career for a few years.

I had been around long enough to understand how nonprofit interviews go. This was probably going to be very long, they would probably want a writing sample, and I did not have the time to waste if we weren't even in the same salary range, so I decided I would start the interview by asking about money. I will never forget walking into the office, shaking my future supervisor's hand, thanking him for taking the time to have me come in for an interview, and telling him that before we started, I needed to know the salary range for the position we were about to talk about.

Before he answered, he told me that the position was very competitive, that people with a wide variety of degrees and experience had applied, including a lawyer and some PhDs (as if I cared), and then told me that the job would pay between $40,000 to $45,000 per year, plus benefits and vaca . . . I had stopped listening.

I smiled, told him I completely understood, and then I stood up, made a gesture to shake his hand, and said that I didn't want to waste his time because we were not even in the same salary range and I had no flexibility. He laughed. Not in an offensive way, but more like he was caught off guard and was a bit impressed by my directness. He put his hands up in a way that said, "Let's slow down and take a second." He then invited me to sit down and talk about what I would need if I were to be offered the position. He said there may be some flexibility.

I think you might see where this story is headed. I got the job and I got the money I asked for, but I was also instructed not to talk about my salary because technically I would be making more than other people in this position, and in similar positions, who had been with the agency for a while. I'm sure they justified that decision because I had a master's degree, somehow gearing almost all of my graduate research in the very subject areas that this job was seeking to relieve: youth development, systemic racism and inequality, and youth prevention programs. I had already been in charge of designing and reporting on nonprofit programs that were using federal funds. It was true that I was not just the best candidate, but that I was also perfect for the job. And sure, maybe it's true that I brought some unique value that justified the monetary adjustment to my pay. I'm okay with clear, justifiable pay adjustments. But what didn't sit right with me was that I was told not to discuss my salary with anyone else. Which meant that I would sit in meetings with people who had been in the job longer than I had, were working just hard and as long as I was, and yet I was making anywhere from five to ten thousand dollars more per year than my colleagues. I had agreed to be complicit, even though it bothered me, because I didn't have the language, skills, or confidence to advocate for transparency without putting my job, and my livelihood, on the line.

> Where there is an intentional lack of transparency,
> there are inequities.

The hiring process in most companies is wrought with inequities and a lack of transparency. The way we hire, pay, promote, and evaluate people is where a lot of inequities are reinforced, and those inequities break down across race and gender. This is why there is such a pay gap for women—and it is even more exaggerated for Black, Latina, and Indigenous women. But unlike with unconscious bias and prejudice, which can be hard to root out because we sometimes don't even know it exists, pay is something that we can easily fix through antiracist policy and practice. Building an antiracist team is about so much more than building diverse personnel.

> Diversity is really just an expression related to the
> number of variations that exist between people.
> Diversity says nothing about the quality of the
> experience that those people have, or how those
> people are represented among the whole.

For example, even if we take a company that has one hundred employees, and fifty-one of them are not White, some people might say that it is a "diverse" workplace, or even a "majority minority" company (which is a nonsensical word that is used to describe schools and organizations when the numerical majority of students are students of Color). However, as my favorite comedian, and friend in my head, Hari Kondubolu pointed out in his comedic album, *Waiting for 2042*, "That's not how math works."[1] Even if a company were 49 percent White, this doesn't make those people a minority unless all of the other people were exactly the same. More importantly, though, is the question of representation and equity. *This* is the actual goal.

Diversity alone is a quantitative assessment about numbers of people. It does not give us an indication about the quality or outcomes of that experience.

Let's take the same company of one hundred employees. If we ranked them by salary or position in the company, what would we find? There's a good chance that we'd find that White folks (the numerical minority) are overrepresented among the top earners or in leadership positions. What if we look at retention rates of employees of Color? Do they tend to stay with the company for longer or shorter amounts of time on average? Broken down by race, what are the proportions of people who have been fired or laid off? What percentage of applicants are members of the BIPoC communities, and does that percentage stay consistent throughout the hiring funnel? Is this percentage ultimately reflected among employee demographics?

Now that we're clear that we're looking to build an antiracist team, not just a diverse one (having done the work to create a safe space), let's dive into some steps we can take to move forward in building an antiracist team. No matter where you are in your entrepreneurial journey, take a look at these steps and fill in the gaps between your current process and what I'm describing here. You can even go back and do some of these things for jobs that are already filled. You might find benefit in re-onboarding employees who are already working with you.

> Start your hiring process way before you need to make a hire.

Remember what I've said before: urgency interrupts equity. Too often, we make hiring decisions when we're in a pinch because we need help to come in yesterday. This causes us to rush the process of preparing the job, hiring a person, and getting them onboarded because we just need a body who can do the thing we need done. My suggestion is to start this process as soon as you start to realize that you can't do it alone, or as soon as you realize that there are tasks that you're doing that are actually keeping you from more important, revenue-generating activities that are probably more in line with your zone of genius.

Start your hiring process by outlining the types of tasks you need the staff person to be in charge of and what success will look like within the position. You'll want to think about not only the task but also the outcome you want to see as a result of this staff person performing their job well. If they have a multidisciplinary job, where they are responsible for a number of various tasks, think about how much time you'd like them to spend on each type of activity. It is your responsibility as the leader to provide guidance on how you would like them to maximize the hours they are working for you. As you develop the job duties, and description for the job, develop the performance indicators that this person will need to meet in order to demonstrate competence and success. I also suggest that you think about the job ladder that this position is a part of. If the idea is to hire a staff member who will ideally stay with the company for the long term, you can provide clarity to potential candidates about what this position could grow into over time.

Let's say you hire an administrative assistant to support you with managing your inbox, scheduling meetings, managing your personal calendar, and being the first point of contact for inquiries and requests for interviews. You can communicate that this position can grow into an executive assistant position or even an office management position over the next one to two years. By providing an idea about the next job opportunity and the time frame, you'll be able to attract candidates who are a bit more future-focused, and also candidates who might be willing to accept a starting salary that is in your budget, because you're communicating a commitment to growth as the company grows. This doesn't mean the candidate has to take one of these next steps with the company, and it also doesn't mean that there won't be other opportunities within the company that this candidate might be interested in. The goal of thinking through the job ladder is about attracting people who can grow with your company and being transparent about what you hope the future will hold.

EMPLOYEE VS. CONTRACTOR

Consider whether the hire will be an employee of the company or a contractor. This decision should be dictated based on the nature of the job and what you are asking them to do. Because of the rise of the gig economy, there has been an increase in the exploitation of contract laborers who do not benefit from employee protections like workers' comp, unemployment benefits, and paid leave, including Family Medical Leave. Contractors are technically private business operators who are expected to use their own equipment, work on their own time, and operate outside of the normal day-to-day business operations of the company. For the most part, if you need an employee to be available to you for certain hours of the day, expect them to be at standing team meetings, and perform the job according to your internal procedures, processes, and frameworks, the position should be an employee. Contract/employee regulations differ slightly from state to state, so check your local laws if you're not sure whether a hire should be an employee or a contractor. I will say, for the record, antiracist businesses should be doing everything they can to create jobs, and this can be done by determining the correct use of contractor and employee.

COMPENSATION

In your planning process, you'll also want to think about what you can pay and what kind of benefits you can offer your employees. If you are striving to be an antiracist entrepreneur, then there are some things that are pretty universally agreed upon among social justice and DEI practitioners when it comes to work and compensation. Here are some things to consider when putting together your compensation plans:

◼ **Company Minimum Wage.** Despite what the minimum wage is wherever you happen to live and work, deciding on a company minimum wage that is consistent with what advocates describe as a livable wage is the kind of policy that more companies can adopt that would contribute to economic equity for employees. Dan Price, CEO of Gravity Payments, instituted a $70k annual minimum salary in his company in 2015 after an interaction with a staff member who was making way below livable wage in their home base city of Seattle.[2] Even though this was a huge financial risk, Price's position was that if most people were living check to check, he didn't need ten years of living expenses saved in an account. He would make sacrifices and decrease his own salary to $70k in order to fund the initiative.

Now, not everyone has the ability to institute a $70k minimum wage. But you might be able to institute a company minimum wage that is more in line with the actual cost of living than the federal minimum wage standards. In case you need a starting point, in August 2021, Rep. Rashida Tlaib made a call for a minimum wage of $18.00 to $20.00 per hour (around $40k a year for full-time salaried jobs) by the year 2025, which would put us closer to cost of living with inflation adjustments.[3]

▪ **Paid Leave.** I don't know how plainly I need to say this, but paid leave, especially sick time, is a public health issue. If the coronavirus has taught us anything—and I hope that it has taught us many things—it has surely taught us that if someone is sick, they need to stay their ass home. But a lot of people won't, because a lot of people work in places that do not have paid leave, and missing a day, or three, or however long they are sick, would put them in financial hardship. Paying people who work for us, even when they are sick, should be part of our social contract to each other. I employ you, which means that you will designate twenty hours, or forty hours, or however many agreed-upon hours of your time, to work in this company, and you will be paid for reserving that time for work. And in the event you are sick, please stay home, and we will pay you, so that you do not get other employees sick.

Even in our culture of digital work, providing sick time to workers is simply a just cause. Providing people with paid time to care for themselves, or their families, will provide them with the emotional and psychological space they need to be fully present in whatever role they are occupying.

The same argument can be made for vacation time. The United States is notoriously known for having some of the worst practices around vacation time. On average, most employees get fourteen days of vacation and tend to leave about four days on the table on average.[4] Compare this to countries such as France, Germany, and Brazil, which offer thirty days of paid vacation time on average, and employees tend to leave a whopping zero days unused.

Supporting workers not just by providing vacation time, but creating policies that incentivize them to use their time, can support your team's overall well-being and morale. If you're ready to push the norm even more, you can minimize the burden of returning to work after vacations by making accommodations to deadlines and creating collaborative work teams so that time-sensitive responsibilities can be redistributed to others, and so that an employee doesn't return from vacation and have to pay for it by working overtime for the next couple of weeks to catch up.

■ **Health Benefits.** In the planning phase, the biggest decision to make is whether or not you can afford to provide health benefits to your team. Unlike paid time off, I don't think there is a clear answer about whether or not to offer this option, because there are a lot of factors. If you're not in the position to be able to provide 100 percent of health benefits to your team members, it actually might be a better deal in some states to have employees get health care through their statewide health-care exchange that many states rolled out as part of the Affordable Care Act. You can provide a health-care stipend to employees to offset the cost if you are able to. Otherwise, look into health-care options carefully and consider not only the cost of the plan but also the deductibles and co-pays your team will be responsible for.

This research is really key, because it might seem like the obvious answer is to provide health care as a company. However, we have to remember that health care is a system with egregious racial disparities. It might cost your Black and Brown employees more if they participate in your health plan than if they pursue health care through the exchange where they might be eligible for additional subsidies or tax credits. Also, you may have some employees who would like to opt out of traditional medicine altogether and to use a monetary health-care stipend to invest in alternative or naturopathic options that wouldn't be covered under your plan.

Salary, health-care benefits, and time-off policies are some of the employment activities named as foundational necessities in the workplace. Additional things you might consider adding to your benefits package to be a more attractive workplace include professional development budgets, vacation stipends, menstrual leave, and expanded bereavement policies for adoption complications, miscarriages, fertility complications, and even pet loss.

DEVELOP THE JOB POSTING

Now that you know the job that needs to be done, and you're ready to talk about the compensation plan that you can offer the right candidates, you are ready to design the job posting. A job posting is sometimes the first piece of information a person receives about your company, so you want to develop a comprehensive job posting that talks about your company and its culture, contains a complete job description, and features some information about the candidates you'd like to attract. A sample job description is included for you in the resource website associated with this book. The following anatomy of a solid job description is what we use and teach in our programs:

▪ **Company Description.** The first section of your job posting should be a clear statement about your company, your company values, and what your company does. Let people know up front that you are a company committed to antiracism, and include any other causes you're committed to. Tell prospective employees that you are committed to creating a diverse, inclusive workplace, and that you encourage people of all identities to apply.

Don't miss the opportunity to position yourself and take this direct stand rather than letting this sit at the bottom of your page, like it's a footnote Equal Opportunity Employer Statement.

- **Job Description.** This is a short summary of the job that gives readers an insight about how the job works within the larger scope of the company. In this section, you'll communicate how many hours per week this job will require, what position it reports to, what department or team the person will work within, and its potential growth opportunities.

- **Salary/Benefits.** Tell people the budgeted salary or salary range for this position (more on this point below).

- **Duties.** Outline a list of the responsibilities this role will have. This should be an exhaustive list, to the fullest extent possible. Try to minimize the use of the phrase "other duties as assigned."

  Let the applicant know who this job is a good fit for and who it's not. List the qualities that you are looking for in your ideal candidate, and talk about some of the values you want your team members to bring to the table. If you're creating a culture that is inclusive and equitable, let candidates know that you are looking for team members who value inclusivity and equity.

- **Application Instructions with Questions.** Let people know how to apply and give them some questions to answer that will give you an indication of whether or not they are a good fit. For example, we ask candidates to share something about their personal commitment to DEI so we can have a quick gauge on their grasp of the language and how long they've been engaged in their own antiracism journey.

POST, RECRUIT, AND REACH OUT

As I said earlier in this chapter, you're responsible for marketing your products and services in the same way that you're responsible for marketing your place of employment, so from now on I want you to take full responsibility for your hiring pipeline. If you want a diverse, representative team, you need a diverse, representative pipeline. This is where you start to address the lack of representation.

Recruitment and outreach require you to do more than just post your job description on Indeed. Start building relationships with people who can send talent your way. And I'm not just talking about your typical university recruitment tour. That's important, too, but make sure you also have universities that serve large populations of Black and Brown folks like HBCUs (Historically Black Colleges and Universities) and MSIs (Minority-Serving Institutions . . . why the government has not renamed this classification is beyond me). And also, engage your own network of colleagues' companies, your own employees, and don't forget your customers and clients.

You can't sit back and post the job description on your website and hope the best person is going to find it. You have to go to them, ask people to apply, post the announcement on your social media channels, and even talk about the right candidate for the job by going live on social media, if that's part of your regular marketing plan. Check in with your community to tell friends that you're looking for someone great to come and make your company even better.

INTERVIEWS AND TRIALS

Once you've gotten a representative number of applicants, then you move into interviews. If you're noticing that candidates of Color are not moving forward at the same rates of their initial applications, ask why. Is there something that is biased about the process or the way you're evaluating applications? The goal is to end up with a pool of candidates in your first round of interviews that represents the diversity present in your applicant pool. If you don't have diversity in the pool, keep deepening the pool through your recruitment and outreach efforts.

> If you need a number as a reference point, according to the United States Census, White folks represent about 60 percent of the American population. Which means that if you have more than 60 percent of White folks on your team, the team is disproportionately White.

Now, as you do your work to become more inclusive, you can make incremental steps to become more representative over time. Obviously, using national demographics as your benchmark may not be appropriate if you're a team of only two or three people. Other metrics you can use to benchmark your goals include your local demographics, especially if you are a company that works in a physical office, or graduation demographics from university programs that are within the fields for which you're hiring (for example, Black women are among the most educated population in this country while simultaneously underemployed).

Once you have selected the candidates you'd like to move forward, set up interviews with them and lead the interviews with the
same type of space creation we've covered in Chapter 7. Consider
how a company that prioritizes the values that you also prioritize
will conduct their interviews. Ask questions about the candidates'
experience contributing to workplace culture, ask their thoughts
about DEI initiatives, let candidates know that you are working toward being an antiracist workplace, and ask what that means to
them.

These questions, in addition to questions about their experience and skills, will give you an insight into their thoughts on
workplace culture and allow you to determine whether they will
be a good fit. For example, if you say to a candidate that your company supports the Black Lives Matter movement and the candidate responds with "All lives matter," they may not be the best fit
for a job that prioritizes an antiracist workplace. When asking
these types of questions, you're not looking for correct answers.
Not everyone has had the same level of exposure to diversity, equity, inclusion, and antiracism work. But you're looking for red
flags.

In our company, we ask candidates to talk about their comfort
level in working with people of all identities and helping them
unpack their relationship to Whiteness. We need to make sure
that our facilitators and coaches can hold space for all of our clients and can meet them with compassion, but also a loving firm-
ness when we have to hold a line. If someone hasn't analyzed their
own relationship to Whiteness and they feel uncomfortable
talking to White people about these topics, they aren't a good fit,
even if they are excellent facilitators in general or are experts in
their field. Being able to uphold our values and our culture is part
of being qualified for the job.

In some cases, you might ask the final candidates to complete
a project that requires collaboration with other team members, or

something that requires them to work independently, to see if they can self-manage and complete projects on time. These are excellent practices, especially if you institute policies like the No Immediate Fire policies that I'll soon discuss. You want to do your due diligence to understand if a person is a good fit before making that kind of commitment.

One note on this: These tasks should be paid. You are asking someone to spend time doing work for your company that will be a benefit to you in one way or another. Anytime we ask people to provide a service, even if it's as part of an interview process, we should offer compensation. When we don't, we may cause inequity in our process. People who are well resourced are going to have an easier time completing the task than a person who may have to take a day off of work or arrange childcare in order to complete the task. We need to be mindful of what we are asking of candidates and ask whether we are creating an opportunity for one person to have an advantage over others because of their resources or privileges.

HIRING AND ONBOARDING

The last piece of your hiring plan should include making the offer and onboarding your new candidate into the role. Job offers should be clear and provide as much detail about benefits as possible. In the job offer, you should provide information that outlines the costs of health-care coverage, the number of days off and whether there are accrual policies, and that the starting salary is in line with the position offered. Give candidates time to think about the offer if needed, and understand that it's likely that they will have to give a resignation notice to their current employer.

After the offer is accepted, you'll want to have an onboarding plan in place that will accomplish a few key things: 1) help them get to know your company and the people they'll be working with, 2) enculturate them into your company's culture and values, 3) help them understand what success looks like in their role, 4) give them the tools they need to get started, and 5) help them feel supported and like a full member of the team.

I recommend a minimum of a thirty-day onboarding plan that provides enough time for your new staff member to shadow other members of your team, especially those they will work with most closely. Provide them structured time to learn about the technology tools your company uses and learn the policies and procedures that they need to be responsible for implementing. If they are being hired into a role where they will be creating new systems and policies, their onboarding needs to be spent getting to know the CEO of the company and other leaders so that they are creating policies and practices that are aligned with the company's values and commitments.

There is probably no more important expression of your values than the people you choose to be responsible for translating them to your clients, customers, and impact communities. Our teams have the ability to enhance and expand our work across multiple dimensions, but that work will only be authentically equitable if it's rooted in antiracist principles. This work takes time, it takes forethought, and it takes a commitment not only to the people you serve but also to the people you hire.

CHAPTER 10

LIBERATORY LEADERSHIP

In 2009, I was working for a nonprofit organization as a program manager for teen pregnancy prevention programs and teen-parent support programs. After about a year of working at the organization, I applied for a position as a supervisor of a national home-visitation program that helped young people prepare to be parents, teach them about healthy child development, and provide emotional support and mentoring to the family. The position I was applying for had been vacant for six months, and over the course of those six months I had informally taken on some of the responsibilities of the role, including helping the home visitors prepare for appointments with new moms, especially new moms who had difficult home environments. I would connect home visitors and families with other social service providers to access support through my own network of relationships I'd built working and living in the community. Having been a teen mom, I knew first-hand about the support these parents needed.

I was twenty-eight years old at the time, and I was very ambitious. I remember preparing my case for this promotion. I met the qualifications for the job, I knew the agency, and I'd been doing home visiting work myself for years. I was once even a recipient of services from this very program. If anyone understood the importance of the gig and the program, it was me. I dressed up for my interview in formal business attire, even though the executive director saw me every day in my jeans and sneakers, and was prepared to answer any questions she could throw at me. And then things got weird.

The executive director, who was also a teen mom at one point in her life and had overcome serious obstacles to get to where she was in her own career, asked me if I had ever heard of something called the "Peter Principle." I had not.

She went on to explain that the Peter Principle says that we tend to promote people who are the best at the job they are in, but, and this is a direct quote, "that sets them up for failure." Then she told me that I reminded her of herself, and that she appreciated my ambition but that I was young and needed to "wait my turn."

This was a person who I'd looked at as an example of what's possible. Someone who could have been a mentor. Even if she didn't think I was ready for the job, there was an opportunity to give me specific feedback about things I needed to do to grow into this kind of role, but that is not what happened. She didn't even have any actual feedback about my performance in the job I had. She was talking about my hypothetical incompetence in a job that I was applying for, with a heavy dose of explicit age bias.

I started applying for a new job shortly thereafter. I couldn't stay in an organization where I knew the leadership thought I needed to be in some holding pen, waiting for my "turn" for a raise or a promotion. I felt disrespected and embarrassed, and I lost confidence in the older leaders because I wondered if every interaction I was having with them was being influenced by my age, or if my ambition was a liability.

This is an example of oppressive leadership, a style of leading that uses bias, prejudice, fear, scarcity, and power to oppress, marginalize, exclude, exploit, and stagnate those they have influence over.

> Oppressive leaders practice a style of leadership that is rooted in the culture of Whiteness that specifically prioritizes "power over" instead of "power with," maintaining formal hierarchies that value mainstream identities and positions (formal degrees and experience, age, economic status, etc.) in addition to top-down structures.

This is what drives toxic capitalism, which values shareholders and profit over people. This style of leadership is concerned with its own ability to maintain power and control, which can cause leaders who practice this type of leadership to view others as resources and tools instead of people.

> People don't leave jobs—they leave managers . . . and oppressive work environments.

Not all bad managers are oppressive. Some bad managers just lack the training to be good leaders. But in my experience, when people leave jobs (and I've left a lot of them), it's usually because oppressive practices were a factor in the company.

If you're doing the work to become antiracist and build a diverse, inclusive, representative team, you also need to reevaluate the way you lead that team and your company so that you can retain your people. You need to provide them an opportunity to thrive, grow, and expand their own expertise; contribute to the company in a meaningful way; and feel honored, respected, and appreciated for their contributions.

In 2021, Basecamp, a well-known and industry-leading tech company, received a lot of attention for releasing a set of new company policies that included dissolving any committees, including the barely formed diversity, equity, and inclusion committee; banning any discussion about social or political issues on the company's internal communication platform; retiring 360 degree employee reviews; and retiring what they identified as "paternalistic benefits," which included wellness programs, farmers market shares, and continuing-education benefits. In addition to these policies, cofounder Jason Fried wrote that the responsibility of negotiating "moral quandaries" should be returned to the cofounders—two cisgender, White, wealthy men.

In Fried's statement, posted on his public blog, he noted the policy was to support "not forgetting what we do here" and elaborated that Basecamp makes "project management, team communication, and email software. We are not a social impact company." He then went on to say that they are not responsible for solving "deep social problems."[1] The irony is that it turned out that these policies were not actually the result of internal tensions about the world's social problems. The trouble was actually Basecamp's internal practices. The Verge, an online media outlet, spoke with several Basecamp employees who confirmed that concerns over Basecamp's culture stemmed from its own practices, including a long-standing practice in which some staff members kept a list of "funny names" of customers that included many African and Asian names. Employees started to point out that this practice was inherently racist, leading to internal tensions, which finally resulted in the policy changes.

Shortly after these policy changes were made, employees started to push back about the negligent leadership and disrespect of employees since the policy changes were announced on a public blog, which is where employees first found out about the changes. Basecamp then offered six months of severance pay to any employees who wanted to leave the company. Thirty percent of Basecamp's team took advantage of the offer, and several of them announced their departures on Twitter, citing the policy changes.

> Your team is not "lucky to have a job."

This is one of the things I've heard oppressive leaders say when they want to justify the poor working conditions they are providing. If you see your ability to employ someone as being a matter of luck for your employees, this is a sign that you have a toxic relationship to your own power. The truth is, if you have to hire someone, maybe many people, it's probably true that you can't run the company alone. And if you didn't have employees, you wouldn't be able to fulfill your commitments to your customers. So, your ability to hire and someone else's need to be employed is actually a mutually beneficial relationship. It's also likely that if you find good talent, your company will perform better; which ultimately benefits the companies owner, and anyone sharing in the profits of the company. It sounds like the lucky ones are the people who are benefiting the most from the labor of the people they employ.

> The message that your team is lucky to have been hired is an intentional manipulation.

WHAT IS LIBERATORY LEADERSHIP?

Liberatory leadership is a leadership style that is rooted in antiracism and the advancement of the collective. This approach to leadership centers justice, transparency, responsibility, and participation, and it uses the power it carries to lift up, empower, include, and create opportunities that cause people to increase their self-determination, self-efficacy, and, ultimately, freedom. Liberatory leaders respect the mutual relationship between themselves, the company, and their team, and they hold a deep appreciation for everyone's participation in making the work happen, which is extended to all employees, customers, clients, audience members, fans, email list subscribers, social media followers, and other contributors.

Liberatory leadership is a radical act because it requires us to be accountable to our power instead of exploiting it (oppressive leadership) or rejecting it (negligent leadership). Some of us, especially those of us who come from direct community work, want to distance ourselves from the power we hold. We might say things like: "I'm just a regular person," "I don't want you to think of me any differently even though I got promoted," or "No need for things to change in our relationship." I believe the intention here is to be humble and let people know that we don't want our position and power to influence the relationship in a negative way. But the fact of the matter is that power changes relationships.

If you are in a formal leadership position, or a situational position where you hold the power for a particular part of the process (as I described salespeople having in Chapter 8), and you dismiss that power, you're ignoring your influence and abdicating your responsibilities to step up and lead.

This might happen when someone is uncomfortable with power because they aren't comfortable with giving directions or delegating responsibilities to others. It could be that they have had bad interactions with leaders in the past and they don't want to replicate toxic, oppressive leadership, so they overcorrect by being too hands-off in their own leadership approach. But negligent leadership is not healthy for businesses.

> When no one is taking full responsibility for leading
> the company or team, it means that no one is holding
> the vision for where the company should be heading
> or providing oversight to make sure that all efforts
> are contributing to the same goals.

Oppressive leaders, on the other hand, are holding their own vision for the company so tightly that they aren't willing to let other people be a part of creating it with them. They can also believe that if they are not in control of every function and task, the vision and goals won't be met. This desire to control everything might be because the leaders believe that they personally have all of the answers, and they need to make sure that people are doing their jobs the "right" way. Those who practice this type of leadership are much more likely to view people as disposable and easily replaceable, to be micromanagers, to not be open to critical feedback, and to cultivate a culture of fear, tension, and toxicity.

Liberatory leadership, however, is about pushing the boundaries of business leadership. It is about creating policies that protect equity and antiracist strategies so that the policies and practices of the company continue beyond any single leader and can be instituted by other staff members with confidence and clarity. We can institutionalize antiracism through what I call the three Ps of an antiracist business: policy, procedure, and practice:

1. **Policy.** Policies are the written guidelines that you create to run your company. Policies are antiracist when they are written to explicitly prevent the exploitation, oppression, and marginalization of all people, and when they reduce the likelihood that people can make leadership decisions influenced by personal bias or identity-based discrimination. Policies are equity-centered when they consider and address the needs of all parties involved,

rather than protect the best interests of the company alone.

2. **Procedure.** Procedures are the protocols that you create that instruct your team how to implement a policy or task that relates to day-to-day business operations. Procedures are important to enforce policies, ensure that new and existing team members have formal expectations for key aspects of their jobs, and keep delivery of programs and services consistent. Procedures are anti-racist and equity-centered when they consider the best ways to deliver consistently high-quality services to clients with a diverse set of needs and identities.

3. **Practice.** Practice has to do with how the procedures and policies are implemented on a day-to-day basis, and how leadership creates norms that scaffold the successful implementation of the policies and procedures.

Here are some examples for how these policies, procedures, and practices can be put into action:

▪ **Policy:** You create a policy that says you don't start an interview process until you've reached a minimum of 20 percent non-White qualified applicants.

▪ **Procedure:** Then you create a procedure that indicates that applications are reviewed two weeks after the initial posting, and you use the demographic data that you collect to determine whether you've hit your goals for representation of people moving into the next round. If you do not have sufficient representation, you implement your recruitment and outreach plan that requires HR, or whoever is hiring to repost the job, to run ads for the posting, send it to HBCUs and HSIs, and make direct requests to potential candidates to apply. Once you have 20 percent non-White candidates to interview, then you move on to the interview process.

◼ **Practice:** Team members verify and realize that the initial round of applicants does not meet the diversity goal. Team members open up the project management list for hiring and find the recruitment and outreach strategy. The team implements all items on the list, and the candidate pool increases from 10 percent to 15 percent. The deadline for making the hire is approaching. The leadership team convenes to discuss whether the recruitment plan was implemented with integrity. The leadership team believes that the plan was implemented, decides to make a new plan to identify a BIPoC recruitment firm for future hiring, and moves forward with the interviews because they feel a good-faith effort was made.

We know that sometimes policies and procedures are not implemented with fidelity 100 percent of the time. Having clear ways to evaluate your policies, procedures, and practices helps you see how they work together, and gives you space to identify where you need to make improvements. These incremental improvements become a part of revised policies and procedures so that you don't have to repeat mistakes or continue to run into the same roadblocks as you institutionalize the lessons.

LIBERATORY LEADERSHIP PRACTICES

There are ways to actualize liberatory leadership into your daily operations. This isn't about feel-good posters on the office walls; it is about concrete decisions and actions, with the guided intention to liberate all peoples and processes within our current economic system and political structures.

Like the Butterfly Effect, small actions can have
global consequences when repeated across a species.
The more we apply these practices and imbibe them
with our full humanity, the sooner we will reach an
antiracist future.

Now for the small actions:

- **Equity Teams.** An equity team is a group of people who meet regularly to create, drive, and support the company or community-wide equity initiatives. These teams receive specialized training to sharpen their equity lens, and apply that lens to the company's operations, roles, projects, policies, procedures, and practices in order to hold the company accountable and provide checks and balances on decision making. An equity team might be responsible for creating a strategic equity plan, evaluating the hiring recruitment and outreach process, planning affinity groups, looking at data about retention and promotion, and addressing accessibility issues. The team members also become advocates for the work in their day-to-day roles and are able to support team members in thinking about their jobs and projects with a lens for equity, inclusion, accessibility, antiracism, and representation.
- **Information and Power Sharing.** Liberatory leaders pull back the veil on their decision making and planning processes and find opportunities to democratize decision making whenever they can. Liberatory leaders realize that a lack of transparency breeds inequity, so they encourage collaboration, communication, and transparency. This may mean that leaders are honest about pivots they are considering, how these pivots might impact people's jobs,

and they communicate the need to cut spending in advance of the action needing to take place.

▪ **Non-negotiable Starting Salaries and Pay Transparency.** Liberatory leaders make decisions to avoid the inequitable practices within other companies by testing dynamic and radical policies that eliminate concerns about disparities related to identity. Non-negotiable salaries—along with other initiatives, including clear metrics for raises or pay differentials—reduce the chances that employees' compensation packages are influenced by their identities.

This can be done by including the non-negotiable starting salary in your job posting and paying that salary no matter what. Letting people know that your non-negotiable policy is part of your equity strategy helps reinforce your commitment. Salaries can be increased if the staff member meets certain objectives or contributes to the role in unexpected ways. Instituting clear policies and practices will help create pay equity in your business and set an example for others about the possibilities for pay equity and transparency.

Consider, for a moment, if an HR professional made a mistake and emailed a document that included details about every single person's pay raise and position. Would you, as the CEO, be able to stand behind those paychecks? Would you be proud to see that Black and Brown folks, and women and nonbinary folks, were all paid the same average salaries as White men? Would you be able to justify pay differentials between people in different or similar roles? Or would people find that pay was distributed arbitrarily and was based on which candidate was the best negotiator?

Do people with the same roles have comparable salaries, and are their pay differences based on equitable metrics? For example, if one person is paid more because they have a degree, does this that mean the person's time and work is worth more than someone else performing the same role? If you say yes, consider whether you are reinforcing a narrative that centers people who have the privilege to attend and finish college.

There are times when pay differentials are appropriate and when formal education does bring something that is distinctly valuable to a role. For example, if you are hiring a master's level social worker, you might pay someone who is a licensed clinical social worker more than someone who has not completed their license, because the licensed person has certain responsibilities that the unlicensed person doesn't have. But in the case of a salesperson who holds a bachelor's degree in psychology and a salesperson who has not completed college, there is no actual difference in their ability to perform the job that the degree inherently provides.

Pay transparency does not need to mean that everyone sits around the table and discloses how much money they make. It means that you are transparent about how you come to decisions about compensation, and that you are transparent about the starting rate of jobs in your company.

■ **No Immediate Release Policies.** This policy basically states that a company will not immediately release an employee unless there has been some sort of egregious, illegal act including theft, violence, or overt harm. This is a policy that protects workers from arbitrary decisions, and even when there is a justifiable reason to release an employee, the policy and supplementary procedures protect the employee from being fired with no warning or financial safety net.

I am a fan of no-fire policies because I have seen too many instances where people contribute to building a company and are fired with no notice or support, and are placed in harm's way. Here is how our own no-fire policy is built.

If an employee is underperforming in their role, there are early conversations about the employee not hitting their KPIs, and training and support is offered to the employee. Ultimately, if they are still underperforming, the employee is given a different job. They can be assigned to a job with less responsibility and pay, or they can be brought down to part-time work, or you can build a transition plan with the employee so they can find another place to work over the course of four to six weeks. This process should never be a surprise to the employee; they are being communicated with at several points beforehand in order to try to motivate them to improve their performance. They are transitioned out only after other attempts have been made, and if they continue to not be a good fit in the role.

Transitioning out can look like the employee being offered a severance package of four to six weeks if you feel that their being part of the company is more of a liability than an asset. Or you can post the job and begin the hiring process while the employee begins to look for other work. You can offer job coaching, writing referrals highlighting the areas of work in which they thrived, while they continue to complete tasks within the company.

I know that this pushes the boundaries of what we consider to be "boss" responsibilities. But if we think about the relationship between people, and remember that business is personal, we can see that firing people without providing notice basically means that you see them as disposable and that you are not considering how this decision, which you have the power to make, is going to affect someone's life.

When employees leave jobs, we ask them to provide a resignation notice. In some cases, companies create policies that specify that if an employee leaves before they give sufficient notice, they can be penalized by the company. The company can decide not to provide a reference for the employee, not to pay out the employee's bonuses, or to make the employee ineligible for rehire. If we expect employees to give us notice if they are leaving, why shouldn't we give them notice if we are planning to ask them to leave? These expectations are inconsistent, and they favor the person who holds the formal power.

It is worth mentioning that adopting this kind of policy creates a more urgent need for hiring practices that take time so that you can find the right people, provide them with test projects to make sure they are a good fit, check references, and really do your due diligence so you can feel confident in the commitment you are making.

▪ **Reimagined Work Schedules.** Increasingly, companies are reimagining how they work, and for how long employees should work. Having a standard nine-to-five job is antiquated and often arbitrary for a lot of companies. Mark Takano, a California congressman, recently introduced legislation that would reduce the legal workweek from forty hours to thirty-two hours over four days.[2] He has stated that many government agencies and private companies have piloted these practices with great success.

Shorter workweeks give people more time to pursue their own interests and spend time with family, and they minimize the need for employees to take days off during the week, according to Takano's proposal.

You can also build in practices such as "protected time" or "no meeting days" to help employees have dedicated, uninterrupted hours to accomplish tasks that require deep focus. Or you can institute periodic breaks or short "sabbaticals" where people are paid to have time to engage in learning opportunities or tinker with new ideas that could offer innovative solutions toward the business's goals.

■ **People over Profit.** Liberatory leaders have to be focused on profit, especially since liberatory leaders want to pay people equitably and offer great benefits packages. But they balance the profit margin and revenue goals with a focus on service, impact, and self-care. Liberatory leaders should not only invest in their own self-care, but they must realize that modeling healthy work/life balance, or work/life integration for their teams, and encouraging team members to practice self-care is actually good for business. Having employees who are not burned out, who engage in their own personal development, and who have community anchors, hobbies, and outside work activities that they feel connected to is good for the well-being of team members. Leaders can model this by practicing their own self-care, community connections, enrichment activities beyond work, and letting the team know that our work doesn't define us.

■ **Representation Goals.** Liberatory leaders will take a stand about the goals related to their diversity, equity, inclusion, and antiracism practices and will attach measurable outcomes to those goals by tracking and reporting on the information. Goals that liberatory leaders might make include representation goals for race and ethnicity in the company at various levels of leadership;

demographic goals for vendors; diverting percentages of revenue or profit to philanthropic initiatives that center marginalized communities; and leveraging their own power to demand diversity and representation at events, speaking engagements, and business opportunities with potential collaborators. Liberatory leaders also understand that there is no perfect formula for accomplishing antiracism goals. Working with experts who get to know your company and support you in developing a strategic equity plan will help you form goals that are best suited for your particular business and are based on your particular journey.

▪ **Tracking Qualitative and Quantitative Data.** Liberatory leaders look for evidence that their efforts are effective and that they are reaching their holistic goals. It's one thing to track revenue, conversions, profit margins, email list subscribers, retention rates, and so on, but it's an entirely different thing to start tracking how quantitative metrics fall across demographic lines. Liberatory leaders want to make sure that their efforts and impacts are representative and consistent. They also want to make sure that clients, customers, and employees are satisfied with the services being provided.

Rolling out customer surveys that measure the actual impacts of your services and products is one way to start understanding the impact of your efforts, but you can go a lot deeper if you set up systems to analyze the data by subgroups, including age range, race/ethnicity, location, socioeconomic status, and so on. Not all of these measures will be appropriate in every company, but sitting with the question "How do we know we're doing a good job, beyond our revenue?" will help you start thinking about other metrics you can measure to get feedback.

CHAPTER 11

MAKING AN IMPACT

One of the most dreaded responsibilities that nonprofit leaders can have is writing grant reports. I can't tell you the number of times that I spent putting together a last-minute survey for program participants after getting an email from the grants department that notified us that we had a report due in two weeks. In fact, one of my favorite trainings to deliver to my early consulting clients had to do with program design and grant reporting, because this process is such a nightmare for so many people. But I digress . . .

What started to really strike me about the whole grant reporting process was just how much it was a total waste of time; it was really just meant to be a measure of accountability between the funders and the nonprofit. In the report, we needed to share information about how all the money was spent, down to the last dollar. The report had to include how many people we served, as well as some basic demographic info about those people, including race, age, and zip code. How many times we provided the service, some general feedback about what happened in the program, and how clients felt about the service. Very few funders actually asked for information related to how the program impacted people. And not one of the agencies I worked at actually took the time to analyze the data.

We would write grant reports, send them to funders, and never look at them again or discuss the outcomes of the report. But everyone wanted to talk about all the impact they were making. "We served four hundred people," "We had a 98 percent attendance rate," and my ultimate favorite was the high school that touted "a 100 percent college placement rate of their entire graduating class." I'm not saying that any of these things are bad, or wrong, but they are kind of misleading and are frequently exploited by marketing departments to position the agency in a positive light.

When I found myself in the consulting and coaching industry a few years later, I noticed a very similar way of talking about making an impact that didn't sit well with me.

> "Impact" started to become one of those marketing catchphrase words that people throw around to try to communicate their commitment to change or forward progress.

Instead, "make an impact" became code for "get more people on your email list," "land more speaking engagements," "sell more products," and "enroll more people." And, yes, I can understand how that is *one* way to talk about impact, but it doesn't actually speak to the quality of the impact a person is making. It's in this lack of transparency—or gap between the dimensions of impact—that inequity can be found.

A great example of how the term "impact" can be misleading at worst, and incomplete at best, is the high school that celebrates their 100 percent college placement. It is a great marketing

186 ■ THE ANTIRACIST BUSINESS BOOK

message to share, especially since these days inner-city schools are competing for students through application and lottery systems, so schools promoting that all of their students were accepted to college can be a strong "selling" point. But it's important to understand that this data point tells us very little about the school or the progress of the students. In fact, it's only a measure of the work the school staff has done, and not about the impact on the students. The school was able to help their graduating class apply and be accepted to college, and as someone who has worked in many schools, I know that this is not an easy thing to do. There are a lot of coordinating details with students and parents that have to be accounted for in order to accomplish this. But here is what the data point does not tell us:

■ How many students got into four-year schools?
■ What percentage of students only applied and were accepted to the local community college that has a guaranteed acceptance policy for any student with a high school diploma or a GED?
■ How many of these students actually registered for classes and showed up for school?
■ How many of them were ready for college-level work without remediation?

And the most important question to ask for any antiracist practice:

■ Are there racial and/or socioeconomic disparities between these outcomes?

If we're not looking at racial and/or socioeconomic disparities between our outcomes' measurements, we are not focused on equity or antiracism.

Here are some other questions we might ask using our antiracist lens:

- Who decided that 100 percent college acceptance was this important?
- If a student did not want to apply, or had no interest in attending college, what was that conversation like?
- Did the students have the ability to exercise self-determination? Or was the application to school connected to a grade or a graduation stipulation? How do we feel about that practice?

Here's what this all comes down to. If you say your company makes an "impact," you're not communicating anything significant because it's really a neutral statement unless used with a lot more context. "Impact" on its own is not inherently good or bad. It just expresses that there is some sort of cause-and-effect relationship but does not express the quality of that relationship. So, if I say, "That person made a real impact on my life," that can mean that the person had a positive effect or a negative effect. But there's a real opportunity in our ability to understand the kind of impact we make, and can make, in moving toward uplifting our business operations, improving our products and services, increasing equity, and practicing our antiracist commitments. But in order to properly measure and articulate impact, we have to be willing to really look at our efforts, analyze them, be honest about what they mean, and share them with our communities.

DIMENSIONS OF IMPACT

A few years ago, I started to play with this concept of the "dimensions of impact" to teach people about the different levels of cause-and-effect relationships so that they could better understand how their work impacted others, how to communicate the impact honestly, and how to measure this impact and use the information to improve practice over time. The goal of thinking about our impact in a few ways, including the dimension, duration, and depth of the impact we create, can help us plan our efforts in the following ways:

1. Be intentional about the impact we want to make, and how we assess that impact.
2. Be critical about assessing the impact that others say they are making.
3. Understand that there are different ways we create impact.
4. Help us be clear and honest about communicating the impact we are making.
5. Learn how to use the information we learn about our impact to improve our practice.

And this is the most important:

6. Create ways to measure our impact, and use this information to make ourselves better.

DIMENSION 1: REFLEXIVE IMPACT

Reflexive impact refers to the outcomes (effects) of our effort (cause) that we personally benefit from or experience. For example, if you sell a product and make one hundred thousand dollars more than your projected sales, you will experience an impact as a result of that campaign. That impact might be that you may need to hire staff to meet the demand for more product, or it could be that you are able to give bonuses to yourself or your team at the end of the quarter.

Outcomes that you measure and report on along this dimension have to do with your reflexive impact related to your own progress, or achievement, and not the achievements of the people you serve, or the quality of your service or product.

Examples of reflexive data points: attendance rates, email list subscribers, open rates, web page visitors, sales conversion rates, enrollment rates in a membership, customer orders, revenue, and number of team members.

DIMENSION 2: PRIMARY IMPACT

Primary impact refers to the direct result (effect) that your product, service, or interaction (cause) has on your intended audience. For example, if you sell fences, the primary impact you have on your customers is related to their experience during the process of deciding to work with you throughout the term of your project and after the project is done. Your client may be impacted positively by the successful installation of a beautiful fence that might increase your customer's satisfaction of their home and outdoor space. It may increase the safety for children or pets that might play inside the fenced-in area, and it may create more privacy for a family who is more introverted or has stronger feelings about home security. These are direct outcomes your customers experience as a result of your services.

Other examples of primary impact data points include business growth of clients enrolling in your business coaching program, new skill-proficiency for clients in a training program, customer satisfaction, and other quantifiable mechanics of goal achievement.

DIMENSION 3:
SECONDARY IMPACT

Secondary impact refers to the indirect impact that other people experience (effect) as a result of the primary impact (cause). In this case, the effect that you have on someone or something else triggers a new outcome. Secondary impacts can be intended or unintended, and they may be more or less relevant to a company based on the company's scope of work.

In my work, secondary impact is incredibly important. I help people improve their businesses, and the cultures of those businesses. We often hear from clients, or employees of our clients, who want to share their experience as a beneficiary of the work we've done with a client. If you sell a product or deliver a service that is not intended to have a secondary impact, this may not be something that matters to your operations or cause.

Other examples of secondary impact include: Your clients' children experience more time with their parents because the parent is able to work less as a result of your support with time management. You run a gift shop and are able to help your clients find the perfect gift for their friends' birthday. As a result of your work effort curating unique gifts and getting to know your clients' needs, your clients' friends experience a stronger sense of closeness or affirmation.

DIMENSION 4:
SOCIAL IMPACT

Social impact refers to the change efforts that we make with or through our businesses, or personal lives, that contribute to a larger social change or movement. In this case, you alone are not fully responsible for impact, but you are a partner or contributor in a broader effort.

TOMS shoes are a great example to demonstrate the differences between primary and social impact, especially when a primary desire seems to have a social cause attached to it. TOMS's primary impact goal is to sell shoes, and to donate one pair of shoes for every pair that someone purchases. It might seem like donating shoes is a social-impact effort, but a 2016 study found that the social impact of this program is negligible.[1]

Researchers at the University of San Francisco found that although recipients of the shoes reported high levels of usage and satisfaction with the shoes, the donation program didn't decrease the overall amount of "shoelessness," or create a significant improvement in foot health, or decrease foot injury. However, TOMS's primary impact goal—to make sure these kids had access to shoes, used them, and liked them—was achieved, and the secondary impact of TOMS's effort was that they inspired other companies to adopt similar models and increased participation through in-kind philanthropy.

What is exciting about these findings is that it gave TOMS shoes an opportunity to evaluate their impact and make adjustments. In their 2020 impact report, TOMS shared their plan to move away from their in-kind model and move toward giving one-third of their profits to grassroots efforts in three core impact areas: ending gun violence, increasing access to opportunities, and promoting mental health awareness.

Other examples of social impact include increasing access to basic necessities like clean water, food, and education; supporting voter registration initiatives; participating in mentorship initiatives; or designating financial grants or jobs for formerly incarcerated people who are reentering their communities.

DIMENSION 5:
POWER/POSITIONAL IMPACT

"Power/positional impact" refers to the impact we have as individual people by virtue of who we are or the position we occupy, in addition to the power we hold. Asking people to be aware of their positional or individual power is a call to mindfulness and self-awareness so that we can mitigate unfair or inequitable biases that might exist just because of the space we occupy. For example, if I am a CEO and I ask for employee feedback about the work environment, the power differential might impact the accuracy of the feedback I will receive. Having an awareness of this power imbalance can lead me to create an anonymous method of collecting employee feedback, or to form initiatives that promote trust with employees, like creating policy protections that allow employees to be open and honest without the fear of retaliation because of the position or power I hold.

Any arena where you hold a mainstream identity, or a role that privileges you or grants you more formal power than others, your power or position is potentially influencing the outcomes of the interaction. We don't have to search very far to find examples of this. Talk to any Black or Brown family about the impact that a uniformed police officer has on them during a traffic stop. Even before there is any interpersonal interaction between the two parties, Black and Brown folks can describe the physiological and psychological impacts that the officer is having on them.

Another example of this might be the impact of receiving a message from your supervisor that simply says, "We need to talk," or "Come to my office first thing in the morning." For some people, these kinds of messages can trigger high levels of stress or anxiety because there is a lack of transparency, and one person holds more power over the other.

This final dimension is included in the impact framework for antiracist practitioners because it's a tool that can help us keep our privilege in check. It can remind us of the invisible, interpersonal effects that we have on others because of our role, identity, status, or proximity to power that can result in actual outcomes in other people's lives.

> Antiracist and equity-centered practices aim to mitigate the exploitation of power, especially if that power is coming from inherent aspects of our identities.

DURATION AND DEPTH OF IMPACT

Duration and depth of impact have to do with the amount of time our outcomes last (duration) and how significant of an effect our impact has created (depth).

How many times have you been to a conference and listened to an incredible speaker who shared an inspirational story that made you emotional and motivated to take action, but by the following Monday the impact of that speaker started to fade, and you got caught up in your day-to-day life, and eventually you couldn't even remember the speaker lineup?

In this example, you may have felt a significant and deep emotional impact, but the impact did not endure. This means that there was a high degree of depth but minimal duration. On the other hand, you may have attended the same conference and learned a new way to organize your time or perform a task at work that saves you about two hours a week on administrative tasks. If you implement that skill, it may have endured in the long term but may not necessarily be a life-changing skill. This would be lower in depth and higher in duration.

It's important to mention that not every business, product, or service is intended to make a long-term impact, or a significantly deep or life-changing impact. The point is to be clear and intentional about what kind of impact you want to make, create strategies to hit your goals, measure your impact for efficacy and equity, and improve your impact over time. What I've found is that entrepreneurs who are on antiracist journeys find great comfort in this deeper understanding of impact because it allows them to clarify their objectives and efforts. It takes the pressure off of trying to determine whether their efforts are actually making a difference, because they engineer their impact and outcomes as intentionally as possible.

MEASURING YOUR IMPACT: OUTCOMES VS. SATISFACTION

A colleague of mine used to say during every training he conducted: "If you didn't measure it, it didn't happen." Now, I don't agree with that statement 100 percent of the time, but I do think that there is a lot of value in measuring your impact. I also believe that the willingness to measure and share your impact can be a part of your accountability and improvement plans for antiracism, DEI, and other customer commitments. Measuring your impact by conducting client surveys, focus groups, and tracking client progress over time is one of the best strategies you can use to identify gaps in your products or service offerings, evaluate the effectiveness and quality of what you deliver, determine the likelihood of your clients and customers being with you in the long term, and build brand trust with a broader audience.

And I'm not talking about your standard customer satisfaction surveys. These surveys typically measure momentary (short-duration) impact but do not ask about the actual outcomes or changes that people experience. Think about the questions that a general customer satisfaction survey typically asks:

- How satisfied are you with the service you received?
- Did the technician arrive within the guaranteed arrival window?
- Would you recommend us to your family or friends?
- On a scale of 1 to 5, how would you rate today's presentation?
- What was your favorite part of the conference?

These questions are fine to ask if the answers are going to give you information you'll need to improve your services, but they aren't the kinds of questions that will provide insight into the duration or depth of the outcomes you've created. When creating marketing campaigns that are honest and aligned, which communicate your impact, you'll want to be able to share real outcomes beyond customer satisfaction. Here is a question that will elicit outcome feedback and tell a deeper story about your impact: How prepared do you feel about your ability to implement the strategy you learned in today's training? This question would allow a company to report the effectiveness of their training workshop. It would also give the company feedback on their training curriculum and format, and potentially identify differences between the effectiveness of their training facilitators. If the question had simply asked, "How satisfied were you with today's training?" we wouldn't be able to make any real assessment on the effectiveness of the program, even if people generally reported that they were satisfied with the workshop.

We can ask similar questions that give us insight into outcomes of customers if we are in a product-based sector as well. Let's take a women's boutique, for example, and ask the following questions:

- Are you a new or returning customer? (this establishes the relationship)
- If you're a returning customer, what brought you back to our shop today?
- If you're a new customer, how did you learn about our store?
- Were you able to find your desired clothes in your size?
- If not, what size are you looking for?
- Do you plan to visit us again?

These questions help us get to know our customers and the experiences they are having in our store. If over the course of six months you find that 40 percent of customers say, "No, I was not able to find clothes in my size," this is an indication that you need to stock more items in those sizes. It's also an opportunity to provide these customers with excellent customer service and offer to place an order and have items in the appropriate size shipped to their house. Alternatively, if 99 percent of your customers say, "Yes, I can find clothes that I love in my size," this can become an honest data point that you should celebrate in your marketing messaging: "We are an inclusive women's boutique carrying sizes 00 to 22. Ninety-nine percent of our customers find clothes they love that fit their body type." Now *this* would be a message to shout from the rooftops.

MEASURING YOUR IMPACT: RACIAL DISPARITIES

I just have to be direct here. If you say that you are an antiracist company, you need to measure your impact and outcomes and analyze them for any racial disparities. This is where we turn up the dial on antiracist practice. Remember, antiracism work is ultimately about life outcomes, and outcomes need to be measured.

It can feel really uncomfortable to ask people to disclose demographic information, especially related to their race, ethnicity, age range, and socioeconomic status, but it's only uncomfortable because we've been taught that we're not supposed to talk about it. Many people grew up with the message that we are all the same, that we should just treat everyone equally, and that we shouldn't see color. Here I am with messages that convey almost the complete opposite: you should, in fact, see color, people are not treated the same, and we need to offer equitable support, not equal support.

> If we have worked to create diversity and inclusion in our business but we are not looking at impact data across the lines of race, we're not fully embodying our antiracist commitment.

You need to be willing to look at how your program and service are impacting different groups of people in order to identify racial disparities. If there is a racial disparity, there is some kind of racial inequity that exists in your business. These are a few ways in which racial disparities might show up.

- Retention rates of Black and Brown employees are lower than those of White employees.

■ Retention rates of Black and Brown customers and clients are lower than those of White customers and clients.

■ Black and Brown clients or customers experience less success with a product or service than White clients or customers.

■ Black and Brown clients have more customer service complaints or critical feedback about the business, product, or service than White customers or clients.

These disparities can exist for any marginalized group, but if we're not asking the questions, we won't see the answers. This is what makes it so convenient for people to share information like "100 percent of our students were accepted to college" without having to disclose that, actually, "100 percent of our students were accepted to college, but only 40 percent of our students were accepted to four-year universities, and 80 percent of those students were White." These statistics are just examples, but they are representative of the kinds of actual disparities that exist within businesses. Antiracist practice encourages us to confront and fix these kinds of racial disparities within our own companies.

You don't have to be an antiracism expert to contribute to dismantling racism.

A lot of clients I meet with will often say something like, "I want to be antiracist, but I don't want our company to turn into an antiracism education company." The pressure to be part of the solution to dismantling racism and White supremacy is high these days. It feels like we are supposed to speak up on every issue or have the right answers about every social problem that arises. I am not asking that anyone pivot their business to become the antiracist educator in their company or become an expert on these topics. That's not the goal.

You may not even have a deep desire to take on a major social issue with your business, and I want to be clear that this is fine too. I'm not saying that every antiracist business has to develop some grand plan to change the world. That's too much responsibility for anyone to take on. Your dream might be to open up a bakery and make beautiful cupcakes for people living in your community. The impact you might want to make is simply to make products for customers in your community who can have them at special occasions. You might want to customize your cupcakes' design to match the style and theme of the customers' occasion so that they can feel like your desserts are part of the art and decor of their event. Amazing. If that is what you feel called to create, do that (also, who doesn't love cupcakes?).

No matter what business you're in, you can still practice antiracism. You can practice antiracism in your hiring processes by creating clear and transparent hiring processes. You can identify Black and Brown vendors and invite them to submit a proposal to be your primary vendor for ingredients. You can create an internship for high school students, or hire people who have faced barriers to employment. You can make it clear that you believe that #BlackLivesMatter, and that you are happy to make cakes for weddings or celebrations for LGBTQIA2S+ families.

Antiracist business and entrepreneurship are pieces of a larger racial justice and equity puzzle that requires the collective efforts of entrepreneurs and leaders, corporate employees, teachers, healthcare workers, policy makers, voter rights advocates, food justice professionals, activists, writers, lawyers, laborers, and union workers, among others. People are working to take antiracist practice into all these areas of life, and together we will shift our culture.

CHAPTER 12

MY LOVE LETTER TO COACHES

In 2019, when I started thinking about writing a book, I thought I'd be writing a book for coaches and personal development entrepreneurs about the need for more impact-driven business practices in the coaching communities. I thought I'd be writing a coaching book because, in 2019, even though I had been doing diversity, equity, inclusion, and antiracism work for a long time, I didn't think there would be demand for the content.

Actually, let me rephrase that: In 2019, before the pandemic, and before the social uprising around the movement for Black Lives in response to the murder of George Floyd, there was not the same demand for this content. I had spent years screaming from the back of the house that there was a fire, and I was warning the industry that the fire was inevitably going to rage.

When I attended my first WDS conference in 2015, I was relatively new to the coaching, personal development, and online business world. I had been listening to some podcasts, picking up some books, and starting to imagine a life where I could leave my nonprofit job and be a full-time entrepreneur. At WDS, I met my first business coach and signed up for my first business mastermind later that year. It changed my life and the trajectory of my path because I fell in love with coaching and online business in a whole new way. I had already completed an intensive coaching certification program and I had spent years studying the science of mentoring and transformation in my grad school programs, but it was WDS and the subsequent community that opened once I started to meet online coaches that really impacted my life.

What I experienced throughout my time in various coaching programs was the need to spend a lot of time listening to the advice that coaches would give me and filtering out the messages that didn't apply to me, or that I didn't have a cultural context for. It took extra effort to find the nuggets of information, here and there, that I could use to help me advance my business. A lot of those skills are things that I've since abandoned because they are misaligned with my values, and I realized they were rooted in systems of Whiteness that I couldn't perpetuate.

> But I also found coaching to be incredibly transformational, and I know that high-quality coaching, consulting, facilitation, and mentoring can change the outcomes of a person's life, a community, a workplace culture, a family's money story, and so much more.

Then I realized something amazing. Coaching and antiracism work have shared goals. I've said this in the book a few times, but it's worth repeating. The goals of antiracism work are about improving life outcomes for Black, Brown, Indigenous, and other marginalized communities. This work is about getting to a world where life outcomes are no longer linked to race. Coaching is about improving life outcomes for anyone who is engaging in the transformational process. The challenge is, much like in the field of mental health, that coaching is often counter to the culture of many Black and Brown communities. The idea that someone would pay another person, tell them their problems and goals, and get advice to move forward is not only a foreign concept, but it's also often dismissed and even discouraged in these communities.

One of my dreams for my work is to get more people trained as certified coaches, especially people who do not identify as, or have a desire to be, a "professional coach." I'd love to see more certified equity-centered coaches in schools, in community organizations, and workplaces so that coaching is more broadly accessible and applied in nontraditional settings, allowing the benefits of coaching to be experienced by more and more people.

The other goal is to help professional coaches become more equity-centered in their coaching practice. It's important to know how to run a business and make money. I think I've made my case for that in the previous eleven chapters. But we've gotten to a point where coaches are overinvested in training on business, marketing, and sales, and underinvested in their own professional practice as a coach. The practice of coaching evolves all the time. Equity-Centered Coaching takes the practice of coaching just as seriously as the success of one's business. In order to help clients achieve their goals, coaches need tools to address human motivation, trauma-informed practice, consent, and how to wear different hats for different roles, such as a coach, facilitator, consultant, and mentor. Most importantly, equity-centered coaches learn how to hold space for a wide variety of diversity in identity and needs in order to provide consistent, high-quality, culturally responsive services.

And I say all of this because it's not happening. So many coaches have jumped on the revenue train, instead focusing their efforts on flashy numbers, five-figure months, six-figure years, seven-figure launches, and this has simply caused a lot of harm.

Throughout 2020 and 2021, I've been a part of too many conversations about clients who have joined programs only to be gaslit and spiritually bypassed, or who didn't receive any actual coaching, but instead were provided with a road map and one-size-fits-all solutions to their business problems. I take issue with this because it's tainting the work and turning people away from the industry. And these people could really benefit from high-quality coaching.

The other thing I take issue with is what I have been calling "show-biz coaching," which I define as a segment of coaches who are focusing on their own celebrity, bringing large numbers of people together, and spending ridiculous amounts of money on events to provide "edutainment" instead of actual mentorship. These people have been doing it for years. Tony Robbins's work is a perfect example of this. He brings thousands of people together for seminars where they become psychologically and emotionally exhausted over the course of weeklong twelve-hour days. He performs "interventions" where he coaches people, some with histories of severe trauma, and asks them to disclose these things in public, with no regard for the consequences. And he is probably one of the wealthiest coaches out there. But this is not what it will take to bring us closer to an equitable world, and it's certainly not antiracist practice.

If you are a coach, you have a life-changing skill that can be used to create real change and contribute to equity, but here's the thing—you can't do it unless you have an understanding of antiracism.

> Because we still live in a discriminatory world where inequities break down along race and class lines, any attempt to help people transform their lives needs to maintain an awareness about how race, class, privilege, and marginalization show up in and shape our lives. These factors will be present for people no matter

204 ■ THE ANTIRACIST BUSINESS BOOK

> what kind of coaching techniques you give them, and
> a coaching practice that is not taking these things
> into consideration is negligent in the same way that
> a physician would be negligent if they didn't consider
> medical history. Unfortunately, our race and class are
> preexisting conditions that influence our lives, and
> if your work is about helping improve lives, then you
> need to understand the full context.

I wanted to include this note for you, dear coaches, because you have been here with me on this journey since I offered the first Diversity and Equity for Coaches course in June 2018, teaching about DEI and antiracism specifically for coaches and personal development industry companies. And you have been part of the *That's Not How That Works* podcast and through 2020 when the fire I had been warning people about exploded in the coaching and online business communities. And, finally, you have witnessed our launch of the Institute for Equity-Centered Coaching, where we began to offer certification programs for coaches and leaders who are committed to an antiracist practice.

I'm really proud of many of you. I often see posts on Instagram that say, "Where are all the people at who made commitments to antiracism?" after many DEI educators saw their online followings decrease or the enrollment decline for their paid communities. It's true; a lot of people who became fired up about the work in 2020 have moved on in 2021. But I still see the deep commitment of so many of you every day. The people who do show up consistently do the work, take accountability for their actions, engage in repair processes, change their policies and practices to reduce the chance that more mistakes will be made, and have become advocates for long-term change. I know you are there, and I appreciate your effort.

And to the Black and Brown folks in my communities, especially Black women who have shown up, who have allowed me to mentor and support you, referred me and my work to others, been in community with me over the years: I love you all. I honor the space you trust me to hold for you, and the space that you create for others.

CONCLUSION

Thank you, reader. I deeply appreciate you for picking up or downloading this book, and for getting this far. I hope you've felt inspired to take some action. Maybe even to learn more. Hopefully, you've been able to relate to some of the stories and ideas I've shared and some of the critiques I'm making about the status quo. I hope you were drawn to this book because you're looking for another way to lead, or maybe you're looking for language to express feelings that you've had but haven't been able to put into words.

I see you.

I spent a lot of time in nonprofits feeling frustrated about procedures and practices that were incongruent with company values, not to mention my own ethos. I've worked with equity institutions that had inequitable policies and offered blanket remedies to problems that were nuanced. I could see that the nonprofit industry would benefit from some of the innovations in new-school entrepreneurialism. I also could see that profit-driven entrepreneurs were disconnected from social issues and the day-to-day realities of people living in the margins. My goal in this book was to bridge these two worlds (to bridge all the worlds) and anchor all business ventures (for-profit or otherwise) in anti-racism work so that we can all work toward economic equity, opportunity, and collective liberation.

The basic fact remains: the vast majority of people interact with businesses on a daily basis—whether it's our own workplace, one of the many places we make purchases from, or the variety of service providers we use, including doctors, repair people, domestic aides, or schools.

> If everyone were using an antiracist framework to manage their companies, we'd all be better off because we'd be invested in each other's humanity.

I firmly believe that success and social progress are not zero-sum goals. I reject the idea that in order for one person to be liberated, another person has to give up their freedom. I reject the idea that we need to choose between making lots of money, living our dreams, and doing work that makes a difference and changes the world. This kind of all-or-nothing thinking has no place in equity or antiracism work. We need to hold space for the belief that we can make the world a better place through our antiracism practices, and other activist pursuits, while also living an abundant life and enjoying the experiences the world has to offer us: great food, fabulous vacations, and plenty of space to be with our friends, families, and communities.

> And, yes, equity may require White folks, as well as other folks with power and resources, to redistribute wealth and resources. The reason that White folks hold this status is because at one point in time (whether four hundred years ago, or yesterday), it was intentionally withheld and stolen from others. And we have all picked up the tools to continue to perpetuate that exploitation.

Building an antiracist business is a radical act, and I know that not everyone will take it on. Some of you may not have the ability to implement some of these suggestions because you aren't the only decision maker, or you don't have influence over a particular policy or practice. Some of you might be part of big institutions where making even the slightest change is a complex task. And some of you just aren't ready to take some of these steps. That's okay. But what steps can you take? Are you willing to look everywhere from the corners of your businesses to the boardroom conference tables to find the places where inequity, oppression, exploitation, and racism live?

My advice is not to wake up tomorrow and rewrite your company handbook. Don't announce a new policy at tomorrow's staff meeting, and definitely don't rush to your website to quickly post an antiracism statement. I am asking you to consider making some decisions that, in some cases, might have a major impact on you and your team working together and relating to each other. I'm asking you to consider policies that fundamentally challenge some of the actions you've been taking throughout your whole career. Neither of us should expect that this book will prepare you for a complete overhaul overnight. That is not how sustainable, responsible change happens. What I want you to do is share this book with a team member, or a colleague, or your business bestie, and talk about it. I want you to talk to more and more people about these ideas and really wrestle with the concepts. I want you to identify what feels easy and aligned, and what feels like it will take more time to integrate, if at all. I want you to make sure that every choice you make is held up against your values and commitments.

I want you to be able to stand behind your choices and understand how they are contributing to a more just world.

I know that I'm asking you to do difficult things, but you have done tough things before, and you will do them again.

If there is one thing that you take away from this book, I hope that it has helped you see something that you will never unsee again: the ways that our "normal" business practices disrespect people. I hope you see the ways that people often exert their power just because they can. I hope your tolerance for arbitrary rules and policies declines, and that you can no longer not notice. I hope that you are self-aware and humble enough to acknowledge when you are the perpetrator, even when you didn't mean to be, and that you are committed and disciplined enough to view it as an opportunity to practice and improve, rather than letting shame, fear, or pride get in the way. You're making choices every day about how you respond to people, how you behave, whether you are upholding unjust policies or processes, or whether you are disrupting and creating a new way. Be a disruptor. Show up. Because we are all we've got.

ACKNOWLEDGMENTS

The first set of acknowledgments I need to make are to my family. The sacrifices made so I could be a wild child and the ambitious woman I've grown to be are many.

To Tito, who has been my partner for the last sixteen years. Thank you for constantly reminding me of who I am meant to be. I truly can't see how I'd be here without your guidance, support, and love.

To my parents. Thank you for never giving up on me and for doing whatever you could to help. And thank you to my siblings for being my biggest fans.

To my kids, my boys, who have been endlessly patient as I finished high school, college, and graduate degrees, and worked days, nights, and weekends to build a better life. Thank you for giving me purpose when I wanted to give up.

To my book coach and editor, Kristen McGuiness. Thank you for helping me shape my ideas and experience into this book. It was such a pleasure working with someone so dedicated to the values and message of this book.

To Rebekah Borucki, president of Row House Publishing, for being an advocate for my work and making me one of Row House's first published authors. I am honored to be a part of this.

To Patty Gift for starting me on this path by asking, "When are you writing your book?" Thank you for encouraging me and introducing me to my agent, Wendy Sherman. Wendy, thank you for guiding me through the early days of this project. I've learned so much from both of you.

To my community, those who have helped shape my life and work. My friends, colleagues, and team members who stayed up talking with me late into the night, commiserated about our frustrations with the world, celebrated our successes, participated in my wild ideas, and encouraged me to take action, even when I didn't feel ready.

To my clients and members of our online communities learning from my team and me over the last few years. Choosing me as your teacher, coach, and mentor on some of the most sensitive and personal topics is genuinely humbling and not something I take lightly.

Thank you, all.

NOTES

INTRODUCTION

1. adrienne maree brown, *Emergent Strategy: Shaping Change, Changing Worlds* (Edinburgh, Scotland: AK Press, 2017).

CHAPTER 1

1. bell hooks, *The Will to Change: Men, Masculinity, and Love* (New York: Atria Books, 2004).

CHAPTER 2

1. Ibram X. Kendi, *How to Be an Antiracist* (New York: Random House Large Print, 2020).
2. Thomas Craemer, "Estimating Slavery Reparations: Present Value Comparisons of Historical Multigenerational Reparations Policies," *Social Science Quarterly* 96, no. 2 (2015): 639–55.
3. "The Freedmen's Bureau Records," National Museum of African American History and Culture, https://nmaahc.si.edu/explore/initiatives/freedmens -bureau-records (last accessed June 2019); Miranda Booker Perry, "No Pensions for Ex-Slaves: How Federal Agencies Suppressed Movement to Aid Freedpeople," *Prologue* 42, no. 2 (2010), https://www.archives.gov /publications/prologue/2010/summer/slave-pension.html.
4. "Jim Crow Laws," History.com, February 28, 2018 (updated March 2021), https://www.history.com/topics/early-20th-century-us/jim-crow-laws.
5. "Black Codes," History.com, June 1, 2010, https://www.history.com/topics /black-history/black-codes.
6. Danyelle Solomon, Connor Maxwell, and Abril Castro, "Systematic Inequality and Economic Opportunity," Center for American Progress, August 7, 2019, https://www.americanprogress.org/issues/race/reports /2019/08/07/472910/systematic-inequality-economic-opportunity/#fn -472910-10.

7. Danyelle Solomon, Connor Maxwell, and Abril Castro, "Systematic Inequality and Economic Opportunity."
8. "FDR and the New Deal," PBS (n.d.), https://www.pbs.org/tpt/slavery-by -another-name/themes/fdr/.
9. "Fair Labor Standards Act Advisor," U.S. Department of Labor (accessed August 2021), https://webapps.dol.gov/elaws/whd/flsa/screen75.asp.
10. Olugbenga Ajilore, "On the Persistence of the Black-White Unemployment Gap," Center for American Progress, February 20, 2020, https://www .americanprogress.org/issues/economy/reports/2020/02/24/480743 /persistence-black-white-unemployment-gap/.
11. Olugbenga Ajilore, "On the Persistence of the Black-White Unemployment Gap."
12. Christian Weller, "African Americans Face Systematic Obstacles to Getting Good Jobs," Center for American Progress, December 5, 2019, https://www .americanprogress.org/issues/economy/reports/2019/12/05/478150/african -americans-face-systematic-obstacles-getting-good-jobs/.
13. Kathryn A. Edwards, "The Racial Disparity in Unemployment Benefits," RAND Corporation, July 15, 2020, https://www.rand.org/blog/2020/07/the -racial-disparity-in-unemployment-benefits.html.
14. Devah Pager, "The Mark of a Criminal Record," *American Journal of Sociology* 108, no. 5 (2003): 937–975, https://www.journals.uchicago.edu /doi/abs/10.1086/374403.
15. Jocelyn Frye and Danyelle Solomon, "Black Women in the Economy: Black Women, Income Inequality, and the Wealth Gap," in *State of Black Women in the U.S. and Key States, 2019* (Washington: Black Women's Roundtable, 2019), https://www.ncbcp.org/assets /2019BWRReportBlackWomenintheU.S.2019FINAL3.22.19.pdf.
16. Emily Moss, Kriston McIntosh, Wendy Edelberg, and Kristen Broady, "The Black-White Wealth Gap Left Black Households More Vulnerable," Brookings, December 8, 2020, https://www.brookings.edu/blog/up -front/2020/12/08/the-black-white-wealth-gap-left-black-households-more -vulnerable/.
17. "Distributional Financial Accounts Overview," Board of Governors of the Federal Reserve System (n.d.), https://www.federalreserve.gov/releases/z1 /dataviz/dfa/.
18. "May 2018 National Occupational Employment and Wage Estimates United States," U.S. Bureau of Labor Statistics (accessed July 2019), https:// www.bls.gov/oes/current/oes_nat.htm.
19. "May 2018 National Occupational Employment and Wage Estimates United States."
20. William G. Whitaker, "The Tip Credit Provisions of the Fair Labor Standards Act" (Washington: Congressional Research Service, 2006), https://www.everycrsreport.com/files/20060324_RL33348 _ad85f13a3a41cd5fafd56b16338e820ac7136692.pdf.

21. "Fact Sheet #15: Tipped Employees Under the Fair Labor Standards Act (FLSA)," U.S. Department of Labor Wage and Hour Division (accessed August 2021), https://www.dol.gov/whd/regs/compliance/whdfs15.htm.
22. "Student Loan Debt by Race," EducationData, July 25, 2021, https://educationdata.org/student-loan-debt-by-race.
23. Christian Weller, "African Americans Face Systematic Obstacles to Getting Good Jobs."
24. "1921 Tulsa Race Massacre," Tulsa Historical Society and Museum (n.d.), https://www.tulsahistory.org/exhibit/1921-tulsa-race-massacre/.
25. "1921 Tulsa Race Massacre."
26. Michelle Singletary, "Black Businesses Are Fighting for Their Lives. We Can't Afford to Lose Them," *Washington Post*, November 20, 2020, https://www.washingtonpost.com/business/2020/11/20/black-businesses-face-discrimination/.
27. Danyelle Solomon, Connor Maxwell, and Abril Castro, "Systematic Inequality and Economic Opportunity."
28. Olugbenga Ajilore, "On the Persistence of the Black-White Unemployment Gap."
29. Christian Weller, "African Americans Face Systematic Obstacles to Getting Good Jobs."
30. "Increasing Access Benefits Everyone: Health Consequences of Being Uninsured," National Immigration Law Center, August 28, 2017, https://www.nilc.org/issues/health-care/health-consequences-of-being-uninsured/#_edn1.
31. Battalia Winston, "The State of Diversity in Nonprofit and Foundation Leadership," white paper, Battalia Winston website (n.d.), https://www.battaliawinston.com/wp-content/uploads/2017/05/nonprofit_white_paper.pdf.
32. "Confronting the Nonprofit Racial Leadership Gap," Race to Lead, June 17, 2020, https://racetolead.org/race-to-lead/.
33. Cheryl Dorsey, Peter Kim, Cora Daniels, Lyell Sakaue, and Britt Savage, "Overcoming the Racial Bias in Philanthropic Funding," *Stanford Social Innovation Review*, May 4, 2020, https://ssir.org/articles/entry/overcoming_the_racial_bias_in_philanthropic_funding.
34. "Leading with Intent," National Index of Nonprofit Board Practices, 2017, p. 11, https://leadingwithintent.org/wp-content/uploads/2017/09/LWI2017.pdf.
35. Molly Delano Brennan and Miecha Ranea Forbes, "The Governance Gap: Examining Diversity and Equity on Nonprofit Boards of Directors," white paper, Koya Partners, 2019, https://koyapartners.com/wp-content/uploads/2018/12/KOYA_GovernanceGap_FINAL.pdf.

CHAPTER 3

1. Annie Palmer, "Read the Memo Jeff Bezos Sent Amazon Employees About Juneteenth," CNBC, June 19, 2021, https://www.cnbc.com/2020/06/17/read -the-memo-jeff-bezos-sent-to-amazon-employees-about-juneteenth.html.

CHAPTER 4

1. Alison Farrell, "CEO Is Receiving a Bonus as If There Was No Pandemic," *Florida News Times*, April 22, 2021, https://floridanewstimes.com/ceo-is -receiving-a-bonus-as-if-there-was-no-pandemic/229123/.
2. Adam Smith, *The Theory of Moral Sentiments* (London: Printed for A. Millar and A. Kincaid and J. Bell, 1759).
3. "Oligarchy," Encyclopædia Britannica (n.d.), https://www.britannica.com /topic/oligarchy.
4. Momina M. Khan, "The 10 Richest American Billionaires 2021," *Forbes*, April 6, 2021, https://www.forbes.com/sites/mominakhan/2021/04/06/the -10-richest-american-billionaires-2021/?sh=71023f18d981.
5. Heather Cox Richardson, *How the South Won the Civil War: Oligarchy, Democracy, and the Continuing Fight for the Soul of America* (New York: Oxford University Press, 2020).
6. Manisha Sinha, "America's Unending Struggle Between Oligarchy and Democracy," *The Nation*, October 3, 2020, https://www.thenation.com /article/culture/heather-cox-richardson-how-south-won-civil-war-review/.
7. "The Rise of State-Controlled Capitalism," interview with Ian Bremmer, *Morning Edition*, NPR, May 17, 2010, https://www.npr.org/templates/story /story.php?storyId=126835124.
8. "The Rise of State-Controlled Capitalism."
9. John Mackey and Raj Sisodia, "Conscious Capitalism: Unleashing Human Energy and Creativity for the Greater Good," white paper, Raj Sisodia website, 2012, http://rajsisodia.com/img/media-kit/Conscious-Capitalism -Unleashing-human-energy-and-creativity-for-the-greater-good.pdf.
10. Isaac Chotiner, "The Whole Foods C.E.O. John Mackey's 'Conscious Capitalism,'" *New Yorker*, February 22, 2021, https://www.newyorker .com/news/q-and-a/whole-foods-ceo-john-mackeys-conscious-capitalism.
11. Spencer Bokat-Lindell, "Are Black Lives What Really Matter to Companies?" *New York Times*, June 23, 2020, https://www.nytimes .com/2020/06/23/opinion/black-lives-matter-brands.html.
12. Paul Blest, "Leaked Amazon Memo Details Plan to Smear Fired Warehouse Organizer: 'He's Not Smart or Articulate,'" *VICE*, April 2, 2020, https:// www.vice.com/en/article/5dm8bx/leaked-amazon-memo-details-plan-to -smear-fired-warehouse-organizer-hes-not-smart-or-articulate.
133 Andrew Yang, "Humanity is more important than money—it's time for capitalism to get an upgrade," ted.com, https://ideas.ted.com/humanity-is- more-important-than-money-its-time-for-capitalism-to-get-an-upgrade/.

CHAPTER 6

1. "The Franchise Business Model 101—An Introduction," Franchise Business Review, November 30, 2018, https://franchisebusinessreview.com/post/franchise-business-model/.
2. "FTC Sends Checks to Nearly 350,000 Victims of Herbalife's Multi-Level Marketing Scheme," Federal Trade Commission, 2017, https://www.ftc.gov/news-events/press-releases/2017/01/ftc-sends-checks-nearly-350000-victims-herbalifes-multi-level.
3. "Sole Proprietorships," Internal Revenue Service (n.d.), https://www.irs.gov/businesses/small-businesses-self-employed/sole-proprietorships.
4. "S Corporation Definition," Bankrate (n.d.), https://www.bankrate.com/glossary/s/s-corporation/.
5. "Meet the 2021 Best for the World™ B Corps," Certified B Corporation (n.d.), https://bcorporation.net/.
6. Will Kenton, "Nonprofit Organization (NPO)," Investopedia, updated April 29, 2020, https://www.investopedia.com/terms/n/non-profitorganization.asp.
7. "What Is a Worker Cooperative?" Democracy at Work Institute (n.d.), https://institute.coop/what-worker-cooperative.
8. Janet Berry-Johnson, "Corporation," Investopedia, September 11, 2021, https://www.investopedia.com/terms/c/corporation.asp.
9. Gene Marks, "Black-Owned Firms Are Twice as Likely to Be Rejected for Loans. Is This Discrimination?" *The Guardian*, January 16, 2020, https://www.theguardian.com/business/2020/jan/16/black-owned-firms-are-twice-as-likely-to-be-rejected-for-loans-is-this-discrimination.
10. "Minority Entrepreneurs," U.S. Committee on Small Business and Entrepreneurship (n.d.), https://www.sbc.senate.gov/public/index.cfm/minorityentrepreneurs.
11. Jessica Gordon Nembhard, "Racial Equity in Co-ops: 6 Key Challenges and How to Meet Them," *Nonprofit Quarterly*, October 21, 2020, https://nonprofitquarterly.org/racial-equity-in-co-ops-6-key-challenges-and-how-to-meet-them/.

CHAPTER 7

1. B. E. Vaughn, "The History of Diversity Training & Its Pioneers," *Strategic Diversity & Inclusion Management Magazine* 1, no. 1, Spring 2007, pp. 11–16. Reprinted in *Diversity Officer Magazine*, https://diversityofficermagazine.com/diversity-inclusion/the-history-of-diversity-training-its-pioneers/.
2. "No Abolition Without Autonomy," Hasta Muerte Coffee, May 31, 2021, https://hastamuertecoffee.com/nocops/.

CHAPTER 9

1. Hari Kondubolu, *Waiting for 2042*, audio. Original Performance, 2013 (Oakland: Kill Rock Starts, 2014).
2. "The Gravity of 70k," Gravity Payments (n.d.), https://gravitypayments .com/thegravityof70k/.
3. Jeff Spross, "Is There an Economic Case for a $20 Minimum Wage," *The Week*, July 24, 2019, https://theweek.com/articles/854375/there-economic -case-20-minimum-wage.
4. Michelle Baran, "Why U.S. Workers Need to Step Up Their Vacation Game," *Afar*, October 18, 2018, https://www.afar.com/magazine/why-us -workers-need-to-step-up-their-vacation-game.

CHAPTER 10

1. Sarah Todd and Heather Landy, "A manager and an employee compare notes on Basecamp's controversial new memo," *Quartz*, https://qz.com /work/2002100/why-basecamps-culture-memo-is-so-controversial/.
2. "Rep. Takano Introduces Legislation to Reduce Standards Workweek to 32 Hours, Office of Representative Mark Takano, July, 27, 2021, https://takano .house.gov/newsroom/press-releases/rep-takano-introduces-legislation-to -reduce-the-standard-workweek-to-32-hours.

CHAPTER 11

1. Bruce Wydick, Elizabeth Katz, and Brendan Janet, "Do in-kind transfers damage local markets? The case of TOMS shoe donations in El Salvador," *Journal of Development Effectiveness* 6, no. 3 (2014), https://doi.org/ 10.1080/19439342.2014.919012.

inclusion (*Cont'd*)
  see also diversity, equity, inclusion, and antiracism
income, universal basic, 50, 58, 61
Indigenous people(s), 16, 25, 51. *see also* Black/Brown, Indigenous, and People of Color (BIPoC)
indirect costs, determining, 142
individual, honoring the, 47
inequity, 12–13. *see also* disparity
Instagram, 80, 85, 137, 147
Institute for Equity-Centered Coaching, 146
institutional racism, physical spaces and, 108
institutions, systemic racism upheld by, 15–16
integrity, team maintenance of, 73–74
intentional culture
  community guidelines for, 117–21
  and physical space, 30, 111–15
intentionality
  for creating customer avatar, 101
  for values-driven culture, 105
  for workplace culture, 109
intentional manipulation, 172
internal environment, examination of, 42
interpersonal relationships
  for antiracist entrepreneurs, 40–41
  and business, 38–39
  culture change and valuing of, 44–45
  and performative gestures, 41–44
  and re-personalizing business, 45–47
  for solopreneurs, 44
interviewing, for teambuilding, 164–65
"invisible hand" (concept), 54
involuntary servitude, 20

Jim Crow, 19, 20, 22, 25
job creation, 60
job descriptions, 162
job offers, 166
job postings, 161–63
job security, 50
Johnson, Richard, 52
Juang, Linda, 113
Juneteenth, 41–42
just commerce, 59–63

Karen archetype, xxiv–xxv, 16
Kendi, Ibram X., 17, 51
knowledge, compensation for, 137
Kondabolu, Hari, 154

labor market, wealth gap and, 24

Latine people, 16
  as term, xxiv
  wealth disparity for, 25
leadership, 168–83
  investment by, 147
  and just commerce, 61
  negligent, 173
  oppressive practices in, 168–74
  racial disparity in, 28
  self-reflection for, 121–22
  see also liberatory leadership
legal business structures, 103–5. *see also* specific types
leisure, 12
LGBTQIA2S+, xxiii
liberatory leadership, 172–83
  defined, 172–73
  oppressive leadership vs., 176
  in practice, 176–83
  as radical act, 173
life outcomes, race and, 12–13, 17–18
Limited Liability Company (LLC), 104
lived experience, racial disparity in, 9–12
living wage, viable, 50, 60

Mackey, John, 57
manipulation, intentional, 172
manufacturing business model, 92
marginalization, self-sustaining system of, 13
marginalized communities
  and coaching, 201–2
  disparities for, 198
  diversity and inclusion of, 125–26
  reparations for, 43
marginalized labor, White exploitation of, 19
marketing
  and impact, 185–86
  investment in, 142
markets, and common goals, 58
mask-wearing, 44–45
Matsumoto, David, 113
McDonald's, 91
Medicare for all, 58, 61
microaggressions, in sales, 144
Middle Eastern people, 16
mindfulness, of physical space, 109
minimum wage
  company, 158
  mandatory, 50, 58, 61
Minority-Serving Institutions (MSIs), 163
misalignment, 74–75
mission statements, 67

ABOUT THE AUTHOR

Trudi Lebrón is the CEO of ScriptFlip! LLC and creator of the Institute for Equity Centered Coaching. By the time Trudi was sixteen, she had two children and had dropped out of high school—all the odds were against her. Today, Trudi runs a million-dollar coaching and consulting firm, helping entrepreneurs and coaches build antiracist businesses and become equity-centered coaches and leaders through ScriptFlip! certification programs, consulting packages, and executive coaching. Trudi holds a BA in Theatre, a Master of Science in Psychology, and is currently ABD in a PhD program in Social Psychology.